MEASURING
AND
EVALUATING
PUPIL
PROGRESS

By
Richard R. DeBlassie
New Mexico State University

MSS Information Corporation
655 Madison Avenue, New York, N.Y. 10021

55517

Library of Congress Cataloging in Publication Data

DeBlassie, Richard R
  Measuring and evaluating pupil progress.

  1. Educational tests and measurements. I. Title.
LB3051.D39   371.2′6   74-8974
ISBN 0-8422-5184-7
ISBN 0-8422-0434-2 (pbk.)

CONTENTS

Chapter I

INTRODUCTION

The reasons why people engage in writing books are varied, complex, and multiple in nature. Some authors may perhaps be described as being egotistical; others as being masochistic. A few may be called esoteric and theoretical, while others may simply be referred to as wanting to make some major or minor contribution(s) to society at large. Still others, like this author, can hopefully be classified as practical individuals.

There is a multiplicity of textbooks dealing with the area of measurement and evaluation in the field of education. As with authors, these textbooks are varied, complex, and multiple in nature. Some textbooks may be esoteric and theoretical. Some may make major or minor contributions to the field. Others may be categorized as practical in nature. Those current textbooks in the field of measurement and evaluation which can be classified as being practical in nature are, in the opinion of this author, rare and difficult to find.

The author, then, has written this text in an attempt to present to pre-service (student) teachers and inservice (practicing) teachers the essentials of measuring and evaluating the progress of pupils from as practical an approach as possible. He could perhaps be labeled an egotist, or a masochist. Hopefully, he could also be conceived as making a significant contribution to education, and most importantly to those charged with educating pupils, teachers. And finally, it is hoped that he is humble enough to accept the proposition that he has set out to accomplish an extremely difficult task.

It is the position of this author that measuring and evaluating pupil progress are vital aspects of the teaching-learning process. Most students of measurement and evaluation of pupil progress are readily convinced of the importance of having skills in these areas. A major problem, however, lies in the reluctance of many people to deal with mathematical or quantitative indices. Most of us having heard the cliche, "I block out whenever math is mentioned," can readily empathize with these people. Another problem is that of the student's identification with "bad" or "unreal" experiences when subjected to tests themselves during their educational experience.

It has been the author's experience in teaching measurement and evaluation courses to pre-service and inservice teachers that the problems alluded to above can be minimized if the measurement-evaluation process is made practical and applicable to the everyday teaching-learning situation. To paraphrase what pupils are saying today about education, the text in measurement and evaluation in education should be "relevant," "applicable," and "practical" for the teacher. It was this need that encouraged the author to write this text on measuring and evaluating pupil progress in the teaching-learning process.

PURPOSE

The major purpose of this textbook is to provide the pre-service or inservice elementary or secondary level teacher the essentials of the measurement and evaluation process in a concise, clear, and practical way. It is intended primarily for the prospective teacher who is engaged in student teaching and whose program of study calls for a prerequisite or co-requisite course in tests and measurement. It is designed, furthermore, with the intent of showing students how the instructor "practices what he preaches." More specifically, the text is predicated on the assumption that the "educational objectives" mode of operation is a viable approach to the teaching-learning process. One of the author's basic premises is that before a teacher can begin measuring and evaluating pupil progress, he must decide with as much precision as possible what it is he wishes to measure. What he wishes to measure and evaluate is more precisely defined if stated in measurable and observable behaviors.

Based upon these presuppositions, the method of measurement and evaluation of pupil progress on the basis of observable behaviors will be consistently emphasized throughout the text. This philosophy, it is hoped, will prevail not only in the text but throughout the course in which the text is used as a major source.

This textbook will also focus on the practical elements of the measurement and evaluation of pupil progress by emphasizing:

1. The most useful and rudimentary methods of measurement and evaluation with a minimum of complex theory and mathematical computations.

2. Methods and techniques of measurement and evaluation which have been found most useful and relevant to the classroom practitioner on a day-to-day basis.

3. Illustrations of specific items on measurement devices to provide students with practical guidelines for the construction of such measures.

4. The commonality of approaches to measurement and evaluation of pupil progress at the elementary and secondary school levels.

OBJECTIVES

General Objectives

1. To provide prospective and practicing teachers with knowledge and skills basic to the appropriate use of tests and measurements as they apply to the measurement and evaluation of pupil progress in the teaching-learning process.

Behavioral Objectives

Upon reading and completing the text the student should be able to:

1. Demonstrate his knowledge of the four levels of educational measurement by providing a written definition and practical classroom application of each level.

2. Demonstrate his knowledge of educational statistics by correctly computing and interpreting indices for the major descriptive statistics: central tendency (mean, median, mole); variability (range, standard deviation); and correlation.

3. Demonstrate his understanding and knowledge of the major score distributions by correctly identifying, drawing, and describing in general terms characteristics of a normal distribution and negatively and positively skewed distributions.

4. Demonstrate his knowledge of the application and use of major normative scores (standard scores, percentiles, percentile ranks, and grade equivalents) by correctly converting raw scores into normative scores and interpreting them.

5. Demonstrate his knowledge of the concept of validity by defining and explaining, in writing, the differ-

ences between the five major types of validity: face, content, predictive, concurrent, and construct. Additionally, the student will examine various standardized tests and demonstrate his understanding of these concepts by identifying the various types of validity purported by these tests.

6. Demonstrate his knowledge of reliability by differentiating, in writing, the major types of reliability: test reliability and score reliability.

7. Demonstrate his ability to compute statistical estimates of the major types of test reliability: test re-test, equivalent forms, and internal consistency, by correctly solving correlational problems related to these concepts.

8. Demonstrate his ability in the area of teacher-made tests by constructing a test at the level of his student teaching assignment. This test will include true-false, multiple-choice, fill-in, and matching items.

9. Demonstrate his understanding of the process of assembling and scoring objective and subjective examinations by presenting the results of the scoring and analysis of one set of tests administered to a class during his student teaching.

10. Demonstrate his understanding of the difference between standardized and teacher-made tests by listing at least eight criteria that differentiate between the two types of tests.

11. Demonstrate his understanding of standardized tests by defining in writing the various types of standardized tests: intelligence, aptitude, achievement, personality, and interest. He should also be able to list and identify at least two specific types of standardized tests under each of the above areas.

12. Demonstrate his knowledge and understanding of observation and recording procedures by constructing and utilizing anecdotal records, checklists, and rating scales.

13. Demonstrate his knowledge of determining grades from various obtained scores and data (test scores, rating scales, observations, etc.) by assigning grades (3-

week, 6-week, final, etc.) to a group of students.

PLAN OF THE BOOK

On the basis of the previously defined objectives, the book will include the following chapters:

Chapter I   -   Introduction

Chapter II   -   Principles of Educational Measurement and Evaluation

Chapter III   -   Educational Statistics: Describing and Interpreting Educational Measurements

Chapter IV   -   Validity, Reliability, and Usability: Desirable Characteristics of Educational Measurements

Chapter V   -   The Teacher-Made Test: Constructing and Scoring Paper-and-Pencil Tests

Chapter VI   -   Appraising Teacher-Made Tests: Analyzing Test Items

Chapter VII   -   Commercially-Made Tests: Standardized Tests

Chapter VIII -   Other Indices of Pupil Progress: Observational Tests

Chapter IX   -   Evaluation: Grading, Marking, and Interpreting

Chapter II

PRINCIPLES OF EDUCATIONAL MEASUREMENT
AND EVALUATION

The classroom teacher is expected to assume the responsibility for ascertaining the extent to which his pupils are making progress in the teaching-learning process. As an individual who has been placed in charge of guiding and facilitating the educational growth of pupils, he has to provide them with an evaluation of how they are progressing with respect to their intellectual and academic development. The evaluation of pupils is a vital and necessary component of the educational process. In order to evaluate pupils, the teacher must establish methods upon which to base his evaluation. More specifically, the teacher must formulate ways of mesuring the educational growth of his students so that he can evaluate them. Additionally, he must base the measurement and evaluation of pupil progress on what he has taught. A major assumption of this book is that the evaluation of pupil progress can be enhanced by improving measurement procedures used by the teacher. It is assumed, furthermore, that teaching and instruction can be improved by the improvement of measurement and evaluation procedures. This chapter, therefore, attempts to provide a basis for educational measurement and evaluation.

MEASUREMENT, EVALUATION, AND INSTRUCTION

In common parlance, there is a tendency to use the terms measurement and evaluation synonymously. Some people, furthermore, confuse the terms testing, measurement, and evaluation. Dizney (1971) has made the following differentiations between these three terms:

> Roughly, we may say testing deals with the use
> of tests and emphasizes the instrument, as it
> were. Measurement is a process . . . . let us
> simply consider measurement to be a process which
> results in a set of symbols representing selected
> characteristics of things in which we are
> interested . . . . Compared to measurement, the
> process of evaluation is even more complex. It
> has commonly been said that evaluation deals with
> value and quality . . . . Further, evaluation
> suggests a more inclusive process than measure-
> ment, a process which incorporates quantitative
> statements en route to value judgments. (pp. 8-9)

He does, however, indicate that testing, measurement, and evaluation represent an interdependent trilogy and summarizes their definitions and interrelationships in a scheme presented in Table I.

Lien (1971) suggests that the terms measurement and evaluation do not mean the same thing. He maintains that measurement and evaluation involves a three-step process and that each of these phases can be seen by defining three key terms in order:

> Measurement: Collection of data, by both objective and subjective means, to provide evidence for analysis and interpretation (Collection Phase).
> Statistical Methods: Presentation and analysis of data (collected through measurement), preparing it for interpretation (Analysis Phase).
> Evaluation: Including measurement and statistics in the broad sense, but, in and of itself, interpretation of the results to determine how well the pupil has grown toward the goals of instruction (Interpretation Phase). (p. 6)

If we can accept the idea that measurement and evaluation are distinct, yet show a definite interrelationship, let us proceed to establish that they are also integral components of the instructional process. The intimate relationship of instruction and measurement-evaluation activities has been established by Dressel (1954). His listing, reproduced in Table II illustrates the common objectives of these two processes.

The relationship between measurement, evaluation, and instruction is also brought into sharp focus by Lien (1971). He suggests that the teaching process is a cycle, that is continuous, and that it involves a three-step process:

1. What is Worth Teaching? - What is Worth Learning? This refers to the objectives, aims, ends, outcomes, or goals of instruction.

2. How Can it Best Be Taught? - How Can it Best Be Learned? In the teaching process, the second step means that one must think through the methods, techniques, procedures, experiences, and activities to be used.

7

TABLE I

INTERRELATIONSHIPS AND DEFINITIONS FOR EVALUATION,
MEASUREMENT, AND TESTING

Term	Definition	Key Synonym or Synonymous Concept	Reference Point
Evaluation	A process of determining worth or for interpreting information from	Judgment of merit	Educational goals, purposes, objectives
Measurement	a process for gaining a symbolic system to represent characteristics obtained by	Symbolic representation	Trait, characteristics, behavior
Testing	procedures for systematizing observations.	Instruments	Tests, rating scales, observation schedules.

From H. Dizney, Classroom Evaluation for Teachers
(Dubuque, Iowa: William C. Brown Co., 1971). Used
with permission.

8

TABLE II

THE RELATIONSHIP BETWEEN INSTRUCTION, MEASUREMENT
AND EVALUATION

Instruction	Measurement-Evaluation
1. Instruction is effective as it leads to desired changes in students.	1. Evaluation is effective as it provides evidence of the extent of the changes in students.
2. New behavior patterns are best learned by students when the inadequacy of present behavior is understood and the significance of the new behavior patterns thereby made clear.	2. Evaluation is most conducive to learning when it provides for and encourages self-evaluation.
3. New behavior patterns can be more efficiently developed by teachers who know the existing behavior patterns of individual students and the reasons for them.	3. Evaluation is conducive to good instruction when it reveals major types of inadequate behavior and the contributory causes.
4. Learning is encouraged by problems and activities which require thought and/or action by each individual student.	4. Evaluation is most significant in learning when it permits and encourages the exercise of individual initiative.
5. Activities which provide the basis for the teaching and learning of specified behavior are also the most suitable activities for evoking and evaluating the adequacy of that behavior.	5. Activities or excercises developed for the purposes of evaluating specified behavior are also useful for the teaching and learning of that behavior.

From P. L. Dressel, "Evaluation as Instruction,"
Proceedings of the 1953 Conference on Testing Problems
Princeton, New Jersey: Educational Testing Service, 1954
Used with permission.

9

3. How Well Has it Been Taught? - How Well Has it Been
    Learned? This is the measurement and evaluation
    phase of the teaching process. It determines by
    measuring and evaluating how well the pupil has
    grown toward the goals of instruction. (pp. 3-5)

Figure 1 indicates how the teaching learning process
should be considered a cycle and should be regarded as continuous in nature (Lien, 1971). From this Figure one can note
that Step 1 (Objectives) assists in giving direction to
Step 2 (Methods); Step 2 then aids in determining Step 3
(Measurement and Evaluation); Step 3 gives further direction
to Step 1. It indicates, furthermore, that the teaching
process is never completed; rather, it is only changed as
new goals, new methods, and measurement and evaluation
modify the process.

THE NEED FOR MEASUREMENT AND
EVALUATION IN EDUCATION

At this point one might very well ask why the teacher
should have any concern about the measurement and evaluation
of pupil progress in education. According to Lindeman (1967)
the measurement-evaluation process can help answer such
questions as:

1. What are the characteristics of pupils at the time
    they enter the school or school system?

2. Considering the general ability and aptitudes of the
    pupils in a given school system, how does their
    achievement in various subject-matter areas compare
    with that of students of similar ability and apti-
    tude in other school systems?

3. To what extent are the instructional objectives of
    the school and the individual classroom teacher
    being achieved through the various instructional
    processes and methods employed?

4. Which children entering the school system require
    specialized instruction in order to take the fullest
    advantage of their exceptional ability or to deal
    effectively with special learning problems? What
    special instructional processes and methods and
    what special programs must be developed for
    achieving maximum individualization of instruction?

10

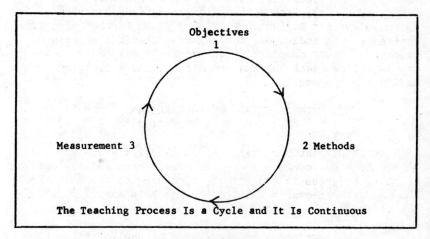

Figure 1. The Teaching Process

11

5. What advice should be given to individual students as they develop educational and vocational plans for the future?

6. How can the student be helped in the development of a realistic self-picture so that he will be able to formulate goals which are consistent with his aptitudes and abilities?

7. How can reasonable achievement levels be determined for each pupil, levels which take into account his general learning potential and his special aptitudes?

8. How can new students be properly placed so that their instruction will be consistent with prior learning and with their aptitudes and abilities?

9. How can information concerning the characteristics of individual pupils be made available in suitable form to outside agencies such as colleges and universities and prospective employers?

10. How can information concerning school programs, policies, and objectives best be gathered and conveyed to parents and other lay members of the community?

11. When more than one method of instruction is available, which one tends to be most effective in maximizing pupil achievement?

12. How can teachers be evaluated so that their talents may be utilized to the fullest and their deficiencies corrected? (p. 7)

In a more declarative fashion, Biehler (1971) lists the potential advantages of the measurement-evaluation process:

1. Evaluation provides feedback, which often functions as reinforcement, which in turn is an essential part of learning.

2. Tests and grades help guarantee that a student will master basic facts and skills en route to mastery of concepts and general abilities.

3. In studying for exams, students usually overlearn. Such overlearning helps assure that materials will be remembered. Furthermore, distortions and faulty

12

generalizations are cleared up when wrong answers are
corrected.

4. Exams require students to try out their ideas under
    rigorous circumstances that limit "fudging." In
    the absence of such control, many students might
    never really test their ideas (or their abilities)
    in a literal sense.

5. Tests and grades may be the only, if not the best,
    way to get many pupils to learn many important things.
    Test scores and grades function as specific goals.
    Most students need incentives even to approach
    their full potential. Sometimes a student who
    studies to pass an exam discovers a new interest.

6. Capable students often thrive on competition. Tests
    and grades may inspire them to work closer to their
    capacity. Specific feedback also permits a student
    to compete against himself.

7. Grades and test performance provide a detailed
    analysis of the strengths and weaknesses of pupils.
    This information can be used in a variety of ways by
    teachers, counselors, and students themselves.
    Evaluation also assists a teacher to improve her own
    performance. In the absence of feedback, it is
    practically impossible for a teacher to make syste-
    matic efforts to change things for the better,
    whereas the very process of writing and reading
    exams aids the organization and presentation of
    subject matter. (p. 381)

CHARACTERISTICS OF EDUCATIONAL
MEASUREMENTS

As indicated previously, measurement entails the collection of data, by both objective and subjective means to
provide evidence for the evaluation process which is inter-
pretive in nature. Measurement devices include statistics,
teacher-made tests, standardized tests, and observational
tools. At this point, it seems essential to examine various
characteristics of educational measurements.

Marshall and Hales (1972) suggest five major characteristics of educational measures:

1. Educational Measures Are Indirect
    Whenever one is attempting to measure a person's

intelligence, to take an example, one cannot weigh it, assess its length, or even see or feel it. How, then, can we measure intelligence? In everyday usage one might say of a person "it was intelligent of him to do that" or "he must lack 'smarts' to do that." In a scientific assessment, experimentally tested behavioral tasks are presented to the individual, and his reactions to these tasks are interpreted as a reflection of his intelligence. Behavior thought to reflect intelligence, rather than intelligence itself, is used as the measure. Thus the measurement of intelligence is indirect. Likewise, behavioral reactions to tasks which are thought to require some specific learning (for example, specific facts or generalizations) in order for a correct response to be given, rather than achievement itself, are used to reflect achievement. All educational and psychological measures of mental processes are indirect. Consequently, whether standardized or teacher constructed, a test is not relevant unless there is a clear relationship between the behavioral tasks of the test and the underlying trait or mental process that the test presumes to measure.

2. Measurement is Incomplete
    From the universe of all the possible questions which one might conceivably write for a test which is being constructed to measure achievement in some area, only a very small number are actually written and selected. If we view the possible items as a hypothetical pool of items for measuring some mental process, we can say that only a sample of items from this pool is actually employed in constructing a test. A test of word knowledge, for example, might have 50 to 100 words in it, but the English language contains thousands of words. Even the most basic vocabulary is thought to contain approximately 4000 words. Not only would the test be incomplete because it employed only a few of the large number of available words, but for each word it would be incomplete in terms of the number of ways the question could have been written. The testmaker must conscientiously endeavor to select behavioral tasks which will be representative of the pool of appropriate tasks for the mental process being measured.

3. **Educational Measures Are Relative**

Let us suppose that Jimmy, a sophomore, answered 50 percent of the items on a history test correctly and missed all the items on a mathematics test. Can we say that he performed poorly in history? Perhaps the history test was very difficult and he did better than all his classmates. What can be said about his knowledge of mathematical concepts? Could you say that he had no mathematical knowledge? What if he were asked "What is 1 plus 1?" These questions cannot be answered from the data furnished, because such measurement is relative. Such measures must be interpreted in terms of some reference group, in this case the members of Jimmy's class who took the examination.

This relative nature of measurement means that we cannot say just how difficult an item is until we try it out on a group of examinees. It also suggests the absence of a true zero score - the score which indicates a complete absence of the trait being measured. Although Jimmy missed all the items on the mathematics test, we cannot say that he has no mathematical knowledge because it is impossible to locate the score point which reflects a complete lack of knowledge. This same limitation prohibits us from saying that a student who got 100 percent right - an erroneous assumption often made when test results are expressed as percentages.

4. **Measures Are Used for Classification**

When tests are administered, measures are obtained for the purpose of classifying people or objects on the basis of some characteristics. When attempting to classify people on the basis of a psychological trait, process, or characteristic, one is normally concerned with continuous data. However, occasionally one uses discrete data when classifying a physical trait. Classification by sex is discrete. Classification by intelligence or weight is continuous. Although we may express weight in pounds, we remain aware that two objects weighing one pound may not remain the same in weight if we refine our measures and include ounces. Likewise, two objects weighing one pound and two ounces may not weigh the same if we refine our scale to measure in tenths of ounces. In fact the characteristic, "weight," is continuous, but superimposed on this continuous characteristic is a scale, in pounds, ounces, etc., which appears to be discrete.

Likewise, achievement is continuous but our measures of achievement, expressed in scores, appears to be discrete. Although all individuals receiving the same score on a test are treated as being the same, we are aware that differences might arise if the instrument were more refined. To summarize, most educational and psychological data are continuous in that the measurement categories can be made smaller and smaller through the refinement of the measuring instrument; however, some data are inherently discrete - refining the scale will not change the size of the categories. For example, the number of apples in a bowl is discrete (unless, of course, one is talking about applesauce!).

5. Errors of Measurement
The measurement of all types of data contain error. If we wanted to determine Clyde's weight we could place him on a bathroom scale and record the weight indicated on the measuring instrument. Would you accept this as his true weight? The measuring instrument may not be accurate for various reasons, including improper tension on the spring, improper calibration between spring and measuring scale, and lack of sensitivity to small weight differences. The observer may not read and record the weight accurately because of a simple error in recording or because of faulty judgment in determining to which of two adjacent weights the indicator is closer. Clyde may just have eaten a large meal, making the measured weight atypical for him. The floor may not be level, causing the indicator to point to the wrong weight. Clyde's observed weight may contain error from several sources: the measuring instrument, the observer, variations in Clyde, and the physical environment in which the measure was taken. These same possible sources of error are present in measures of psychological characteristics and traits. (p. 1-3)

Generally, measurement theory over the years has placed all kinds of measurements into one of four measurement scales referred to as the nominal-ordinal-interval-ratio classification. These four levels of measurement represent characteristics of educational measurements as well.

The nominal scale is characterized by numbers that bear no hierarchical relation to each other but are used simply as labels to designate different kinds or classes of things. The

16

ordinal scale is characterized by a rank relationship between
numbers. We could, for example, designate the winners of a
440-yard dash by the numbers 1, 2, and 3. We can say with
relation to the measure or trait in question that 1 > 2,
2 > 3 and that, therefore, 1 > 3. We cannot say, however, by
how much 1 differs from 2 or 2 from 3. The interval scale
is characterized by the presence of a logical, but arbitrary,
zero point and equal units along the scale. Centigrade scales
for measuring temperature are usually classified as interval
scales. The ratio scale differs from the interval scale in
that its zero point is a "true" zero rather than an arbitrary
zero. True zero means the complete absence of the variable
being measured. Measures of height and weight are examples
of ratio scales. Dizney's (1971) scheme shown in Figure 2
contains an excellent summarization of these four types of
scales.

Educational measurements are also characterized according to the continuous–discrete variable type of classification. In measuring mental and physical traits we are
typically dealing with variables. Variables are simply
defined as attributes or qualities which exhibit differences
in magnitude along points from high to low along a scale
designed to apply this notion. Weight, for example, is a
variable because different objects can assume different
points on a scale said to give "measures" of weight. If
all possible objects weighed the same, the trait of weight
would have no descriptive value. It would not be a variable.
Similarly if all pupils had the same measured intelligence,
intelligence would have no descriptive value; it would not
be a variable.

Most of the variables which we deal with in educational
measurements are referred to as continuous variables. A
continuous variable is one which is capable of any degree of
subdivision. IQ's, for example, are usually thought of as
increasing by increments of one unit along an ability continuum which ranges from low to high (i.e., idiot to genius).
Physical measures (height, weight, etc.) also fall under the
classification of continuous variables: within the given
range any "score" integral or fractional may exist and have
meaning.

Discrete or discontinuous variables, on the other hand,
are variables which exhibit a lack of continuity or real gaps.
A salary scale, for example, may run from $90 per week to
$100 per week in units of $1; no one receives, one may say,
$96.51 per week.

17

Level of Scaling	Formal Characteristics	Visual Representation	Function	Example
nominal	mutually exclu- and identifiable categories	1 2 3	allows classi- fication and description	race: where 1, 2, 3, re- present white, black, brown
ordinal	rank order, more than and less than	1 2 3 4 5 6	allows the above plus ranking	test scores, where 6 is greater than 5, etc., but units repre- sent differ- ing amounts
interval	units have equivalent meaning throughout the scale	1 2 3 4 5 6 7 8	allows the above plus the deter- mination and comparison of differences	elevations from arbi- trarily select points, where units are equi- valent throughout the scale
ratio	meaningful zero	0 1 2 3 4	allows the above plus the deter- mination and comparison of ratios	human heights, where 3' is 1/2 of 6'

Figure 2. Comparison of Measurement Scales.

From H. Dizney, Classroom Evaluation for Teachers (Dubuque, Iowa: William C. Brown Co., 1971). Used with permission.

Blood and Bud (1972) make an excellent differentiation between continuous and discontinuous variables:

> Let us attempt to clarify the difference between
> continuous and discontinuous variation through
> the use of examples. Height is an example of a
> continuous variable. Note that if we use one of
> our usual systems for assessing height, say a
> yardstick, it is theoretically possible for
> things to be placed at any point on such a scale.
> One thing might be placed at the point 2 ft.
> 3 1/2 in. Another might be placed at the point
> 2 ft. 3.34 in., or even 2 ft. 3.3338 in. It
> is also readily apparent that the unit here
> employed to describe height, the inch, is
> capable of infinite subdivision. We may sub-
> divide the inch so far as expedience demands.
> Class size, on the other hand, is an example
> of a discontinuous variable. The unit that is
> used to describe class size is the individual
> student. We say that one class contains 29
> students; another contains 30 students. No
> class ever contains 29 1/2 students. It is
> not possible for a class to fall at any point
> along this scale except at those points labeled
> by whole numbers. Nor can we subdivide the
> unit in any meaningful fashion. Note also
> that the numbers used to describe the size of
> classes are obtained by a process of enumeration
> or counting. We would not apply the term
> "measurement" to such a process. (p. 3)

TEACHER COMPETENCE IN
EDUCATIONAL MEASUREMENT

A previously stated assumption was that the evaluation of pupil progress can be enhanced by improving measurement procedures used by the classroom teacher. It is of vital importance that the competence of teachers to measure educational attainments be improved. Ebel (1961) suggests that to establish the importance of improving teacher competence in measurement, it is necessary to show not only that educational measurement is needed and possible but also that teachers are currently deficient in getting this job done. He identifies seven serious deficiencies possessed by teachers in educational measurement:

1. Teachers tend to rely too much on their own sub-
    jective, but presumably absolute, standards in
    judging educational attainments.

2. Teachers tend to put off test preparation to the last minute, and then to do it on a catch-as-catch-can basis.

3. Many teachers use tests which are too poorly planned, too short, or too inefficient in form to sample all the essential knowledge and abilities in the area of educational attainment covered by the tests.

4. Teachers often place too much emphasis on trivial or ephemeral details in their tests, to the neglect of basic principles, understandings, and applications.

5. Teachers often write test questions, both essay and objective, whose effectiveness is lowered by ambiguity, or by irrelevant clues to the correct response.

6. Many teachers overlook, or underestimate, the magnitude of the sampling errors which afflict test scores.

7. Most teachers fail to test the effectiveness of their tests by even a simple statistical analysis of the test results.

He goes on to say that a teacher who is competent in educational measurement should:

1. Know the educational uses, as well as the limitations, of educational tests.

2. Know the criteria by which the quality of a test should be judged and how to secure evidence relating to these criteria.

3. Know how to plan a test and write the test questions to be included in it.

4. Know how to select a standardized test that will be effective in a particular situation.

5. Know how to administer a test properly, efficiently, and fairly.

6. Know how to interpret test scores correctly and fully, but with recognition of their limitations. (pp. 67-71)

PREVIEW

On the basis of the previous discussion of the principles of educational measurement and evaluation and the necessity for teachers to become competent in these areas, the remainder of the book focuses on helping the prospective and practicing classroom teacher in developing the necessary competencies for enhancing the maximum in measuring and evaluating pupil progress. As such, the emphasis in the remaining chapters is on helping the teacher to develop skills in: (1) using educational statistics; (2) determining desirable test characteristics; (3) constructing and appraising informal (teacher-made) tests; (4) understanding and using standardized tests; (5) interpreting the results of the measures in evaluating pupil growth.

Chapter III

EDUCATIONAL STATISTICS: DESCRIBING AND INTERPRETING EDUCATIONAL MEASUREMENTS

This chapter is intended to expose the teacher to the most frequently needed statistical concepts in as elementary, practical, and realistic terms as possible. Too often the classroom teacher has conceived of statistics as an abstract and abstruse discipline to be avoided at any cost. As a result of this conception, too many teachers have remained both ignorant and frightened of statistics. Consequently, their skills in measuring and evaluating pupil progress have suffered. Statistics represent a major method of presenting, analyzing, and interpreting educational measurements.

WHY STUDY STATISTICS?

Suppose that a classroom teacher has collected some data on his pupils by objective and/or subjective means (measurements) in order to analyze and interpret how well they have progressed toward the instructional goals (evaluation). What are some of the things that can be done to get the maximum information from the results? What can teachers do with statistics? Why should they study and be skilled in statistics? Here is a list of information that can be obtained from a statistical analysis of data (Downie and Heath, 1970):

1. Averages can be calculated. These averages give a picture of the typical performance of the groups.

2. The variability of the measurements can be determined. By using the average as a point of reference, one can determine how scores or observations spread about this central point.

3. Graphs, tables, and figures can be prepared to portray clearly the nature of the group or groups.

4. The "raw" scores can be transformed into a more meaningful form. The most common of these forms are centiles (percentiles) and standard scores. When dealing with classroom performance, raw scores can be changed into letter grades.

5. The relationship or association of one variable to another can be determined. These statistics are called correlation coefficients and are among the

most useful. For example, it might be of interest to find the relationships between an intelligence test and classroom tests; between abilities and interests; or among various measures of physical development. Variables such as age may be related with measures of achievement and with psychological and sociological characteristics.

6. The reliability or consistency of the measurement instruments can be determined. This is done by making two measurements of the same individuals with the same or "paralleled" devices and finding the correlation between the two sets of data. As will be seen, there are also other ways of computing reliability coefficients.

7. The validity or the extent to which the measurements are accurately measuring can be determined. With regard to statistical validity, the correlation between socres made on one test and performance on another measurement, called a criterion, is an index of validity. For example, intelligence tests are often validated by correlating scores on these tests with grade point averages. If the intelligence tests are valid, those who obtained the highest scores will also receive the highest academic grades.

8. One set of measurements, or a combination of variables, can be used to predict future status or behavior. This is probably the major end of all correlation work; in themselves correlation coefficients are of little value.

9. A knowledge of statistics will allow the teacher to read with greater understanding the research literature in his field and that in the area of tests and measurements. It will also enhance the teacher's ability to read and understand test manuals. (pp. 3-4)

ARRANGING MEASUREMENTS AND SCORES

Quantitative indices (measurements and scores) have little meaning until they have been arranged or categorized in some systematic way. Statistical methods may be defined as the presentation, arrangement, and analysis of numerical indices or data collected through various methods of measurement. This statistical analysis of data will lead to evaluation or the interpretation of measurements. The teacher's ability to arrange and analyze measurements statistically will enhance his skills in evaluating pupil progress.

Measurements which the teacher typically deals with are known as raw scores. Raw scores are the first quantitative results obtained in scoring a test (teacher-made or standardized). They usually have little or no meaning for a given student until they can be compared with some reference point which indicates whether they represent good or poor performance. Having obtained these raw scores following the administration of a test, the teacher's task is to determine what to do with the results and how to interpret (evaluate) them.

Let us assume that the raw scores in Figure 3 represent the results of a 100-item teacher-made Biology test. Since most teachers deal with class sizes of 30, statistical methods will be illustrated using this number of scores. The analysis of these scores is identical to an analysis of test scores which an elementary school teacher might also make.

As these raw scores stand, they are of little value in determining what they mean. The following steps should be followed by the teacher in attempting to organize these data so that they can be statistically analyzed and interpreted:

1. Arrange the scores in order of magnitude (rank order scores from high to low).

2. Construct a frequency distribution which is a representation of all the scores, from the largest to the smallest, together with the number of times (frequency) that each raw score occurs.

3. Construct a graphic portrayal of the frequency distribution of scores. This will give a better indication of how the raw scores are distributed. Two types of graphic portrayals of raw scores in a frequency distribution are frequency polygons and histograms.

4. Determine descriptive characteristics of the distribution of scores by computing various numerical indices including central tendency (mean, median, mode) and variability (range, quartile deviation, and standard deviation).

5. Transform the raw scores into a more meaningful form such as percentiles or standard scores.

These five steps comprise the essence of the remainder of the chapter.

ORGANIZATION AND STATISTICAL
ANALYSIS OF SCORES

Rank-Ordering Scores

Figure 4 represents the 30 raw scores ranked in order of magnitude.

The types of information that can be inferred from rank ordering the scores as shown in Figure 4 are still minimal in nature. It can be discerned, for example that the highest score (H) is 98 while the lowest score (L) is 50, and that this represents a raw score difference of 48 (H−L=48). One can work statistical computations with raw scores that have rank ordered, but this is not advisable because of the likelihood of making errors. The advantages of simply rank ordering the data are minimal in nature.

In order to avoid computational errors and the misinterpretation of the rank-ordered raw scores, it is better to organize the data into a frequency distribution.

CONSTRUCTING A FREQUENCY DISTRIBUTION

The steps in setting up a frequency distribution are as follows:

1. Set up a column of numbers under the label score with the top number equal to the highest score and the bottom number the same as the lowest score in the distribution of raw scores. Include all possible numbers between these two values.

2. Set up second column labeled tallies next to the score column. Under this column place tally mark to the right of the score in the distribution.

3. Take the sum of all the tallies for each raw score represented and place this sum in a third column labeled frequency (f). This process of tallying is an intermediate step in constructing the frequency distribution. The results of steps 1-3 are shown in Figure 5. The distribution in Figure 5 is referred to as a simple frequency distribution from which some information can be inferred and statistical computations made. However, it is somewhat difficult

79	50	77	93	60	71
69	66	83	88	61	89
57	68	70	55	74	81
98	84	72	70	82	65
94	53	64	70	76	74

Figure 3. 30 Raw Scores on a 100-Item Biology Test

98 (H)	84	77	71	68	60
94	83	76	70	66	57
93	82	74	70	65	55
89	81	74	70	64	53
88	79	72	69	61	50 (L)

Figure 4. 30 scores on a 100-item Biology Test in Order of Rank

Score	Tallies	f	Score	Tallies	f	Score	Tallies	f
98	/	1	81	/	1	64	/	1
97		0	80		0	63		0
96		0	79		0	62		0
95	/	1	78	/	1	61	/	1
94	/	1	77	/	1	60	/	1
93		0	76		0	59		0
92		0	75	/	1	58		0
91		0	74	//	2	57	/	1
90	/	1	73		0	56		0
89	/	1	72	/	1	55	/	1
88		0	71	/	1	54	/	1
87		0	70	///	3	53		0
86		0	69	/	1	52	/	1
85		0	68	/	1	51	/	1
84	/	1	67		0	50	/	1
83	/	1	66	/	1			
82	/	1	65	/	1			

Figure 5. Simple Frequency Distribution of 30 Raw Scores on a 100-item Biology Test

27

to obtain a reflection of where the scores are spread
out over a range of 48 raw score points (H-L=48).
Additionally, computations are somewhat cumbersome
while the data are in this type of a frequency distribution. In order to minimize these disadvantages
of the simple frequency distribution it is better to
organize the Raw Scores into a grouped frequency
distribution.

4. Set up a grouped frequency distribution. In order to
   organize raw scores into a grouped frequency distribution, we adhere to the following steps:

   a. Determine the range or the difference between
      the highest and lowest scores (R=H-L or R=98-50
      or 48).

   b. Settle upon the number and size of categories
      into which the raw scores will be classified.
      Commonly used grouping intervals are 3, 5, and
      10 since these have been found easier to work
      with in computing statistics. A good rule is to
      select somewhere between five and fifteen cate-
      gories. The number of intervals or categories
      which a given range will yield can be determined
      approximately (within 1 interval) by dividing the
      range (R) by the grouping interval tentatively
      chosen. In our distribution of scores, for exam-
      ple, 48, the range, divided by 5 (the interval
      size tentatively selected) gives 9.6 or 10 to
      the next full integer. A grouping interval of 3
      would have given 16 categories, while a grouping
      interval of 10 would have yielded 4.8 or 5
      categories. An interval of 3 would spread the
      data too much, thus losing the purpose for
      grouping; an interval of 10 with 5 categories
      would make the categories too coarse. A group
      interval or class interval size of 5 was there-
      fore chosen as best suited to the 30 raw scores.

   c. Once we have selected the size of class interval,
      we must then decide which shall be the five
      scores that constitute each interval. A rule of
      thumb is to decide that the lowest score in the
      interval shall be a multiple of the size of the
      interval. In our distribution of scores the
      highest score is 98 and so the top class interval
      limits are 95-99 since the lowest score in the
      interval should be a multiple of the size of the

class interval which is 5. Our top interval,
therefore, would include only the score of 98.
We then proceed to write class intervals down to
the place where the lowest score in the interval
should be a multiple of the size of the class
interval which is 5. The lowest score (50) is
included in the bottom interval (50-54).

d. Tally the scores in their proper intervals. The
    result of steps a. - d. are shown in Figure 6
    which represents a <u>grouped</u> <u>frequency</u> <u>distribution</u>.
    The grouped frequency distribution, then, con-
    sists of the class intervals column (C.I.) and
    the frequency column (f). The sum of the f
    column (N=30) represents a check on the accuracy
    of placing all of the scores into their respec-
    tive class intervals. The M.P., or midpoint
    column will be referred to when we are portraying
    the frequency distribution graphically.

GRAPHIC PORTRAYAL OF A FREQUENCY DISTRIBUTION

In order to obtain a better portrayal or indication of
how the raw scores are distributed, it is generally the
practice to show the scores in graphic or picture form. Two
major types of graphic portrayals of raw scores are the <u>fre-</u>
<u>quency</u> <u>polygon</u> and the <u>histogram</u>.

The steps in constructing a <u>frequency</u> <u>polygon</u> for the
scores in the grouped frequency distribution begin by laying
off some coordinate axes. On the horizontal or X-axis
(abscissa) we lay off an appropriate scale corresponding to
the midpoints of the class intervals. (See Figure 7). Normally, this scale runs from slightly below our lowest score to
slightly above our highest score. On the vertical or Y-axis
(ordinate) we lay off a frequency scale. As a general rule of
thumb (for esthetic reasons) we make the Y-axis about two-
thirds to three-fourths as long as the X-axis. We divide the
Y-axis into equal units representing frequencies. The highest
value on the Y-axis will be equal to our highest frequency.
Having laid off our axes in this fashion, the next step is to
plot the frequencies of each interval above the midpoints of
the intervals on the X-axis. There are two scores on the first
interval 50-54. We therefore place a dot at a frequency value
of two immediately above the point 52 on the X-axis. In the
same fashion, we place dots at the appropriate frequency levels
above the midpoints 57, 62, 67, 72, 77, 82, 87, 92, and 97.
We also place a dot at zero frequency at the two points 47
and 102 so that we can complete the frequency polygon at the

Class Intervals	Tallies	f	M.P.
95-99	/	1	97
90-94	//	2	92
85-89	//	2	87
80-84	////	4	82
75-79	///	3	77
70-74	//// //	7	72
65-69	////	4	67
60-64	///	3	62
55-59	//	2	57
50-54	//	2	52
		N=30	

Figure 6.   Grouped Frequency Distribution of 30 Scores on a 100-item Biology Test

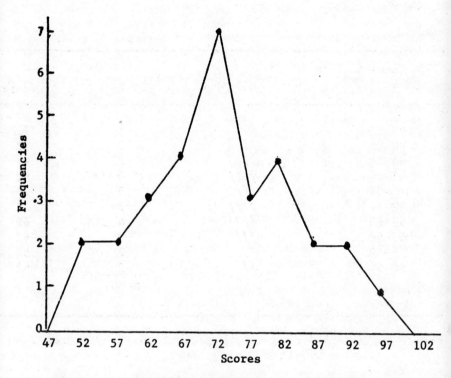

Figure 7. Frequency Polygon for the 30 scores on the 100-item Biology Test.

31

extremes. When all the points have been located on the coordinate axes, they are joined by a series of straight lines to form the frequency polygon indicated in Figure 7.

A histogram or column diagram is constructed by beginning with a pair of axes similar to those used in constructing our frequency polygon. Once we have laid off our coordinates, the next step is to construct the bars that form the basis of our histogram. Beginning with the bottom interval of our grouped frequency distribution, we draw a straight line at the level of the appropriate frequency along the complete length of each interval. For example, for our bottom interval 50-54, we would draw a line at the level of one frequency between the two points 49.5 and 54.5 on our X-axis. Then we would connect this line with the bottom of our scale at the points 49.5 and 54.5. Why do we use these instead of 50 and 54? We refer to the former pair of points as the actual limits of the interval and the latter pair as the observed limits of the interval. The actual limits are so-called because we are dealing with continuous variables. You may recall that in continuous variables, the units of measurement may be infinitely subdivided and that the numbers identifying such units are to be considered intervals rather than points. For example, the number 50, which is the lowest observed limit of our lowest interval, actually represents an interval extending from the point 49.5 to the point 50.5. Similarly, 54, which is the upper observed limit of the same interval, represents an interval extending from 53.5 - 54.5. Our interval, then, really extends from the lower limit of 50, which is 49.5, to the upper limit of 54, which is 54.5. The actual limits of the interval 50-54 are thus 49.5 - 54.5.

We complete our histogram by following the same proce-dure for each interval. The result of this procedure is the bar graph shown in Figure 8 where the total area of the graph represents the total number of scores on our tests, and the area of each bar is proportional to the frequency within that interval.

Garrett (1966) refers to when to use the frequency poly-gon and when to use the histogram:

> The question of when to use the frequency polygon and when to use the histogram cannot be answered by citing a general rule which will cover all cases. The frequency polygon is less precise than the histogram in that it does not repre-sent accurately, i.e., in terms of area, the frequency upon each interval. In comparing two

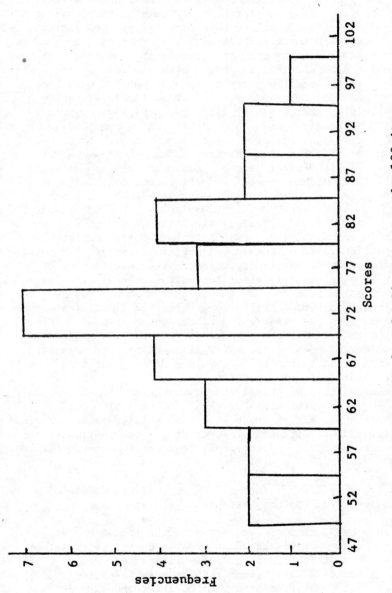

Figure 8. Histogram for the 30 scores on the 100-item Biology Test.

33

or more graphs plotted on the same axis, however, the frequency polygon is likely to be more useful, as the vertical and horizontal lines in the histograms will often coincide.

Both the frequency polygon and the histogram tell the same story and both enable us to show in graphic form how the scores in the group are distributed whether they are piled up at the low (or high) end of the scale or are evenly and regularly distributed over the scale. If the test is too easy, scores accumulate at the high end of the scale, whereas if the test is too hard, scores will crowd the low end of the scale. When the test is well suited to the abilities of the group, scores will be distributed symmetrically around the mean, a few individuals scoring quite high, a few quite low, and the majority falling somewhere near the middle of the scale. (p. 19)

SCORE DISTRIBUTIONS

Much of the description of statistics in analyzing data comes from the types of graphic portrayals represented by the data. The frequency polygon, for example, is widely used in characterizing score distributions. A common way to characterize score distributions is the classification referred to as normal (symmetrical) or skewed (asymmetrical). A distribution is considered symmetrical if its frequency polygon (or histogram) has exactly the same shape on either side of the midpoint (median). A distribution which does not possess identical or nearly identical values is not symmetrical and is referred to as skewed or asymmetrical.

The normal distribution or normal curve is of primary importance in educational measurement because many characteristics of pupils (i.e., intelligence, achievement, height, etc.) approximate a normal form or curve. The major characteristics of the normal curve (bell-shaped curve) are that it has a single mode (high point), extends symmetrically in both directions, and gradually approaches the base line as an asymptote. Interpreted in terms of frequency of scores, asymptote means that the scores are concentrated around the midpoint and gradually decrease in frequency as the distance from the center increases. Figure 9 illustrates the characteristics of the normal curve.

A glance at Figure 9 reveals the following characteristics:

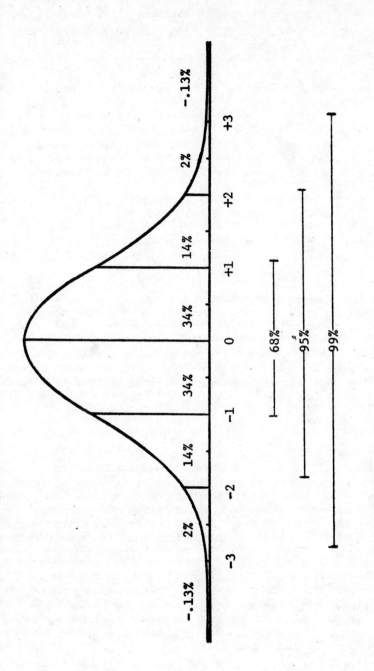

Figure 9. The Normal Curve

1. The curve is perfectly balanced; i.e., the left and
    right halves are equal. Thus, the mean, median, and
    mode have the same value.

2. The tails of the curve do not join the baseline,
    since the limits of the curve are plus and minus
    infinity.

3. Approximately 34% of the cases fall between the mean
    and one standard deviation. By doubling this, one
    will note that about 68% of the cases lie within one
    standard deviation, plus and minus of the mean.

4. Within plus and minus two standard deviations from
    the mean will be included roughly 95% of the cases.

5. Within plus and minus three standard deviations
    from the mean will be included practically all,
    roughly 99% of the cases.

Further reference to the normal curve is made in a later
section dealing with the transformation and interpretation of
raw scores.

There are various ways of labeling and describing score
distributions that deviate from a normal distribution. Ways
to describe such distributions include reference to: (1) the
mode; (2) skewness; and (3) kurtosis.

The Mode

The mode is defined as the most frequently occurring
score in a distribution. Modes can be identified by an
inspection of frequency polygons and appear as those scores
indicated by the highest points. A unimodal distribution is
one with only one mode; bimodal distributions have two modes.
Those distributions with more than two modes are called
multimodal distributions. Illustrations of these appear in
Figure 10.

Skewness

Skewness is defined as a lack of symmetry in a distribution. Asymmetrical distributions may have negative or
positive skews. A method for checking skewness is to compute
the difference between the mean and the median (M-Mdn). If
this difference is positive (greater than zero), the distribution is positively skewed. If the difference is negative
(less than zero), the distribution is negatively skewed.

If the distribution is symmetrical, M—Mdn=0, because the two measures of central tendency have the same value. Skewed distributions are shown in Figure 10.

Kurtosis

Kurtosis is defined as the degree to which a distribution is peaked. A normal curve is <u>mesokurtic</u> in nature. A curve that is more peaked than a normal distribution is called a <u>leptokurtic</u> curve, while a flatter than normal curve is referred to as a <u>platykurtic</u> curve. These types of distributions are also shown in Figure 10.

Dizney (1971, p. 50) enumerates common possible causes for the different types of curves referred to in Figure 10. Table III summarizes these features and their causes.

DETERMINING DESCRIPTIVE CHARACTERISTICS

Once the scores obtained through measurement have been ranked or grouped, the classroom teacher should proceed to determine various characteristics of the group of scores by computing such statistical indices as central tendency (mean, median, and mode) and variability (range, quartile deviation, and standard deviation).

A generic definition of the term central tendency is as follows: <u>Central tendency</u> refers to numerical indices that represent or typify the performance of a group as a whole. The three major measures of central tendency are:

1. <u>Mean</u>. The mean is the arithmetic average or simply the sum of all scores divided by the number of scores. A major property of the mean is that every raw score is used in its computation and contributes its proportionate share to the result. It is usually referred to as the average.

2. <u>Median</u>. The median is the midpoint or middle value in a distribution of ranked scores. It is the point beneath which fall fifty percent of the scores. It is also referred to as the 50th percentile. This measure is not affected by relative size or by extreme scores.

3. <u>Mode</u>. In a set of ungrouped scores, the mode is defined as the most frequently occurring score. In a frequency distribution the mode is defined as the midpoint of the interval having the highest frequency

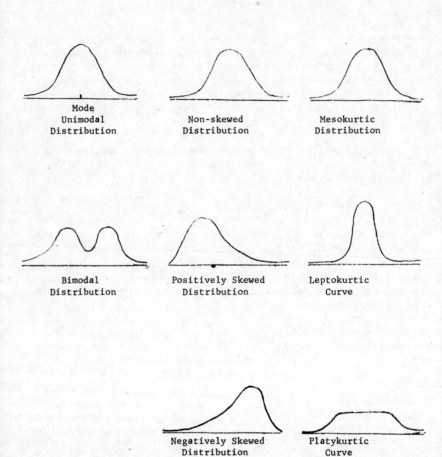

| Modes | Skewness | Kurtosis |

Mode
Unimodal
Distribution

Non-skewed
Distribution

Mesokurtic
Distribution

Bimodal
Distribution

Positively Skewed
Distribution

Leptokurtic
Curve

Negatively Skewed
Distribution

Platykurtic
Curve

Figure 10. Different Types of Score Distributions

TABLE III

GENERAL TYPES OF SCORE DISTRIBUTIONS
THEIR CHARACTERISTICS, AND POSSIBLE CAUSES

Type	Characteristics	Possible Explanation
Positively Skewed	Mode at lower end, decreasing frequencies with increasing scores.	Test too difficult, group deficiencies, poor instruction, or trait is naturally skewed.
Negatively Skewed	Mode at upper end, decreasing frequencies with decreasing scores.	Test too easy, group exceptionally proficient, extraordinary instruction, or trait is naturally skewed.
Leptokurtic	Short range and extreme peak.	Insufficient test length or redundant items, group unusually homogeneous, influence of instruction either constant or superficial, or trait is homogeneous.
Platykurtic	Wide range or flat distribution or both.	Test very heterogeneous in difficulty of items or traits measured, group unusually heterogeneous, instruction very individualized, or trait naturally heterogeneous.
Normal	Unimodal, symmetrical, "bell-shaped," "idealized" mathematical function.	Virtually unkown in its strict form outside of theoretical discourse, approximations possible when traits, tests, and events result in a mode at the center of a distribution with successively fewer frequencies in both directions from the center of the distribution.

From H. Dizney, _Classroom Evaluation for Teachers_ (Dubuque, Iowa: William C. Brown Co., 1971). Used with permission.

of scores. It is possible to have more than one mode in a distribution of scores which represents one of its major limitations. If a distribution has two scores that occur with equal frequency we have a bimodal distribution; if it has three scores equal in frequency, we have a multimodal distribution.

Garrett (1966) suggests when to use the various measures of central tendency:

1. Use the mean

    (1) When the scores are distributed symmetrically around a central point, i.e., when the distribution is not badly skewed. The M is the center of gravity in the distribution, and each score contributes to its determination.
    (2) When the measure of central tendency having the greatest stability is wanted.
    (3) When other statistics (e.g., SD, coefficient of correlation) are to be computed later. Many statistics are based upon the mean.

2. Use the median

    (1) When the exact midpoint of the distribution is wanted - the 50% point.
    (2) When there are extreme scores which would markedly affect the mean. Extreme scores do not disturb the median. For example, in the series 4, 5, 6, 7, and 8, both mean and median are 6. But if 8 is replaced by 50, the other scores remaining the same, the median is still 6 but the mean is 14.4.
    (3) When it is desired that certain scores should influence the central tendency, but all that is known about them is that they are above or below the median.

3. Use the mode

    (1) When a quick and approximate measure of central tendency is all that is wanted.
    (2) When the measure of central tendency should be the most typical value. When we describe the style of dress or shoes worn by the "average woman," for instance, the modal or most popular fashion is usually meant. In like manner, in speaking of the average wage in a certain

industry, we often mean the modal wage under specified conditions. (pp. 38-39)

While central tendency represents numerical indices which represent the performance of the group as a whole, variability is a measure of the dispersion of the scores. More specifically: Variability refers to numerical indices which indicate the manner in which the scores are dispersed, scattered, or spread around their central tendency. The three most common measures of variability are:

1. Range. The range is defined as the difference between the highest and lowest scores.

2. Quartile Deviation. The quartile deviation or semi-interquartile range is defined as one-half the distance between the 75th and 25th percentiles in a frequency distribution. It is a numerical index which represents the average distance between the median (50th percentile) and the first and third quartiles.

3. Standard Deviation. It is a statistic used to express the extent of the deviations from the mean for the distribution. It is obtained by taking the square root of the mean of the squares of the deviations from the mean of a distribution. If the group tested is a normal one their scores, if plotted graphically, would yield a normal distribution curve. Approximately two-thirds (68.3%) of the scores would lie within the limits of one standard deviation above and one standard deviation below the mean. One-third of the scores would be above the mean by one standard deviation, and one-third below the mean by one standard deviation. About 95% of the scores lie within the limits of two standard deviations above and below the mean. About 99.7% of the cases lie within the limits of three standard deviations above and below the mean.

Garrett (1966) suggests when to use the various measures of variability:

1. Use the range
   a. when the data are too scant or too scattered to justify the computation of a more precise measure of variability.
   b. when a knowledge of extreme scores or of total spread if all that is wanted.

2. Use the Q
   a. when the median is the measure of central tendency.
   b. when there are scattered or extreme scores which would influence the SD disproportionately.
   c. when the concentration around the median – the middle 50% of cases – is of primary interest.

3. Use the SD
   a. when the statistic having the greatest stability is sought.
   b. when extreme deviations should exercise a proportionally greater effect upon the variability.
   c. when coefficients of correlation and other statistics are subsequently to be computed. (pp. 59-60)

Measures of central tendency and variability are highly related in that the former are contingent upon the latter for interpretation and use. Before any measure of central tendency can take on meaning, it is important to know in what fashion the scores are spread around it. Freeman (1962) has stated this relationship:

> A measure of central tendency is a single value intended to represent one of the principal characteristics of the group studies. But any measure of central tendency has limited significance in itself, because it is derived from individual scores that may vary considerably. To say, for example, that the mean IQ of a group of children is 115, tells us little about the characteristics of that group. It is essential, therefore to accompany a mean or median by one or more measures of dispersion. (pp. 28-29)

This relationship will be elaborated on later in the chapter.

Computation of the various descriptive measures of central tendency and variability discussed above will now be illustrated. The formulas for computing these measures are shown at the end of this chapter. In order to simplify these computations as much as possible, Figure 11 has been prepared for the 30 raw scores previously alluded to. Computations for these six descriptive measures have been made in terms of both ungrouped and grouped data. Some teachers with class sizes of 30 or smaller may wish to compute these descriptive indices without grouping the scores into a frequency distribution. Other classroom teachers with

Ungrouped Scores

98	84	77	71	68	60
94	83	76	70	66	57
93	82	74	70	65	55
89	81	74	70	64	53
88	79	72	69	61	50

A. Central Tendency

1. Mean = $\frac{\Sigma X}{N} = \frac{2193}{30} = 73.10$

2. Median = $\frac{(N-1)}{2}$ Result = $\frac{31}{2} - 15.5 = 71.5$ Count Up

3. Mode = Most Frequently Occurring Score = 70

B. Variability

1. Range = H-L = 98-50 = 48

2. Quartile Deviation = $\frac{Q_3 - Q_1}{2} = \frac{81.5 - 64.5}{2} = 8.5$

3. Standard Deviation = $\sqrt{\frac{\Sigma X^2}{N} - M^2} = \sqrt{148.81} = 12.2$

   or

   Standard Deviation = $\frac{\Sigma \text{ highest } 1/6 - \Sigma \text{ lowest } 1/6 \text{ of Scores}}{1/2N}$

   $= \frac{462 - 275}{15}$

   $= 12.46$

Grouped Scores (*)

(1) CI	(2) f	(3) MP or X'	(4) fX'	(5) x	(6) fx	(7) fx²
95-99	1	97	97	24	24	576
90-94	2	92	184	19	38	722
85-89	2	87	174	14	28	392
80-84	4	82	328	9	36	324
75-79	3	77	231	4	12	48
70-74	7	72	504	-1	-7	7
65-69	4	67	268	-6	-24	144
60-64	3	62	186	-11	-33	363
55-59	2	57	114	-16	-32	512
50-54	2	52	104	-21	-42	882
			2190			3970

A. Central Tendency

1. Mean = $\frac{\Sigma fX'}{N} = \frac{2190}{30} = 73.00$

2. Median = $1 + \left[\frac{N/2-F}{fm}\right] i = 69.5 + \left[\frac{15-11}{7}\right] 5 = 72.35$

3. Mode = Midpoint of C.I with highest f = 72

B. Variability

1. Range = H-L = 98-50 = 48

2. Quartile Deviation = $\frac{Q_3 - Q_1}{2} = \frac{81.38 - 65.13}{2} = 8.13$

3. Standard Deviation = $\sqrt{\frac{\Sigma fx^2}{N}} = \sqrt{132.33} = 11.50$

(*)NOTE: (a) Columns (1), (2), and (3) under Grouped Scores above represent the frequency distribution of the 30 scores as previously shown in Figure 6.

(b) Column (4) is used when one wishes to compute the mean for grouped data using the formula: $M = \frac{\Sigma fX'}{N}$

(c) Columns (5), (6), and (7) are used when one wishes to compute the Standard Deviation for grouped data using the formula: $SD = \sqrt{\frac{\Sigma fx^2}{N}}$

Figure 11. Statistical Measures of Central Tendency and Variability for the 30 Ungrouped and Grouped Scores on the 100-item Biology Test.

class sizes of 30 or more, may decide to organize the scores into a frequency distribution and compute the descriptive statistics on the basis of this grouping. The statistics arrived at by either method vary but slightly and are quite accurate regardless of the method of calculation.

Before proceeding to the calculations in Figure 11, the student should be made aware of the fact that whenever raw scores are grouped into a frequency distribution, the individual scores lose their identity and are represented by the midpoint of the class interval in which the raw scores fall. To illustrate, raw scores 93 and 94 when grouped into our frequency distribution (see Figure 6) fall in the class interval 90-94. Both scores, therefore, are represented by the midpoint 92 rather than retaining their own individual identities or values of 93 and 94. This will be alluded to again at a later time.

Based on the statistical computations derived and shown in Figure 11, the following descriptive statements and conclusions are made with reference to the 30 scores:

1. The three measures of central tendency (M=73.10, Mdn=71.5, and Mo=70 for ungrouped data and M=73.00, Mdn=72.35, and Mo=72 for grouped data) are highly similar in numerical value and the distribution of scores can therefore be said to approximate a normal distribution.

2. Since the mean, median, and mode are similar in value and hence indicate that the 30 scores simulate a normal distribution, the logical measure of variability is the standard deviation. Since our near-normal distribution of scores has a mean of 73 and a standard deviation of 11 (actually 11.5) we can say that the scores are scattered as follows:
   a. 68% of the pupils taking the test have scores between 62 and 84 (M + SD = 68% of cases).
   b. 95% of the pupils have scores between 51 and 95 (M + 2 SD = 95% of cases).
   c. 99% of the pupils have scores between the lowest score 50 and the highest score 98.

3. Computations of the various measures of central tendency and variability using ungrouped versus grouped scores showed little numberical differences. We can, therefore, conclude that either method of computation is usable and applicable from the class-room teacher's point of view.

4. The fact that our distribution of 30 scores approximates a normal distribution indicates that the Biology Test discriminated well between the high and the low achievers. The Biology Test, therefore, represents a <u>relative achievement</u> test. This will be discussed further in a later chapter.

TRANSFORMING RAW SCORES

Not only should the classroom teacher be interested in determining various descriptive characteristics of the group upon which the raw scores were obtained, but he should also ascertain the relative importance of each raw score. In ascertaining the relative importance of the raw scores, one establishes the position of each score in relation to their distance from the mean and in relation to other scores. Two major types of scores for this purpose are <u>standard scores</u> and <u>percentile ranks</u> which are referred to as derived scores:

1. <u>Standard Scores</u>. Standard scores are scores that are expressed in standard deviations away from the mean. They enable one to compare the scores made by an individual on two or more tests or by two pupils on the same test. There are a number of different standard scores used in educational measurement. Since they are all based on the same principles, only the most commonly used standard scores will be discussed: <u>Z-scores</u> and <u>T-scores</u>.

   a. <u>Z-scores</u>. Z-scores are the most elementary type of standard scores. This score forms the basis for the computation of all other standard scores. It expresses the position of a raw score in terms of the number of standard deviation units a raw score is above or below the mean. The formula for a Z-score is:

   $$Z\text{-score} = \frac{X-M}{SD}$$

   X = raw score
   M = mean of the distribution of scores
   SD = standard deviation of the scores

   In order to become familiar with this formula let us apply it to a few of our raw scores in our distribution of 30 scores. Let us convert the raw scores 98, 84, and 65 into Z-scores:

For 98 $Z = \dfrac{98-73}{11} = 2.27$

For 84 $Z = \dfrac{84-73}{11} = 1.00$

For 65 $Z = \dfrac{65-73}{11} = -.73$

These three scores can then be located on the baseline of the normal distribution curve. Raw curve 98, for example, falls at a point 2.27 σ above the mean, while raw score 65 falls at a point -.73 σ below the mean.

It should be noted that whenever a raw score is smaller than the mean, its Z-score always has a minus sign. It is also possible to obtain Z-score values which are in decimals. These two factors can increase the chances of making serious errors in computations. For this reason Z-scores are infrequently used directly in educational measurement and evaluation. They are usually converted into a standard score system known as a T-score which uses only positive and whole integers.

b. T-scores. A T-score refers to any set of normally distributed standard scores which has a mean of 50 and a standard deviation of 10. T-scores can be obtained by multiplying the Z-score by 10 and adding 50:

$$T\text{-score} = 10(Z)+50$$

$$T\text{-score} = 10\left[\dfrac{X-M}{SD}\right]+50$$

T-scores for the previously alluded to raw scores of 98, 84, and 65 are:

For 98 $\begin{aligned} T &= 10(Z)+50 \\ &= 10(2.27)+50 \\ &= 23+50 \\ &= 73 \end{aligned}$

For 84 $\begin{aligned} T &= 10(Z)+50 \\ &= 10(1)+50 \\ &= 10+50 \\ &= 60 \end{aligned}$

$$\text{For } 65 \quad \begin{aligned} T &= 10(Z)+50 \\ &= 10(-.73)+50 \\ &= -7+50 \\ &= 43 \end{aligned}$$

Since T-scores always have a mean of 50 and a standard deviation of 10, any T-score is directly interpretable. Our T-score of 60, for example, always indicates one standard deviation above the mean; our T-score of 43 is almost three-fourths of one standard deviation below the mean, and so on.

Figure 12 indicates the Z-score and T-score values for the 30 raw scores which will be referred to again following the discussion below on the second type of derived scores commonly used, percentile ranks.

2. Percentile Ranks. A percentile rank is the position on a scale of 100 to which the pupil's score entitles him. It is a numerical index that tells what percentage of pupils within a specified group scored lower than a certain raw score. In our distribution of 30 scores, for example, if the percentile rank corresponding to a raw score of 72 is 50, 50 percent of the pupils in the group had raw scores lower than 72. The formulas for computing percentile ranks from ungrouped or grouped scores follow:

Ungrouped Data
$$PR = \frac{\text{Number of persons below score} + 1/2 \text{ of persons at score}}{N} \times 100$$

Grouped Data
$$PR = \frac{\left(\dfrac{f_p}{i}\right)\left(X - 1\right) + F}{N} \times 100$$

where:

PR = percentile rank
f_p = frequency of scores within class interval wherein scores lie
i = size of class for which PR is sought
1 = actual lower limit of class interval containing raw score
F = sum of the frequencies of all class intervals below
N = number of scores in distribution

47

Raw Score	Z-Scores[1]	T-Scores[2]	Percentile Ranks[3]
98	2.27	73	98
94	1.90	69	95
93	1.82	68	92
89	1.45	64	88
88	1.36	64	85
84	1.00	60	82
83	.91	59	78
82	.82	58	75
81	.73	57	72
79	.54	55	68
77	.36	54	65
76	.27	53	62
74	.09	51	57
72	-.09	49	52
71	-.18	48	48
70	-.27	47	42
69	-.36	46	35
68	-.45	45	32
66	-.64	44	28
65	-.73	43	25
64	-.82	42	22
61	-1.09	39	18
60	-1.18	38	15
57	-1.45	36	12
55	-1.64	34	8
53	-1.82	32	5
50	-2.09	29	0

$$[1] \text{ Z-Score} = \frac{X-M}{SD} \qquad [2] \text{ T- Score} = 10(Z) + 50 \qquad [3]_{PR} = \frac{\# \text{ of persons} + \frac{1}{2} \text{ of persons below Score} \quad \text{at score}}{N} \times 100$$

Figure 12. Z-scores, T-scores, and Percentiles for the 30 Raw Scores on the 100-item Biology Test

To determine the percentile rank of raw score 60 from ungrouped data (see Figure 11) we would proceed as follows:

$$\text{PR for R.S. } 60 = \frac{4 + .5}{30} \times 100 = 15$$

To determine the percentile rank of raw score 60 from grouped data (see Figure 11) we would have:

$$\text{PR for R.S. } 60 = \frac{\left(\frac{3}{5}\right)(60 - 59.5) + 4}{30} \times 100 = 14$$

There are a number of situations that call for the use of percentiles in relation to percentile ranks. One example is in the use of standardized tests. There is a definite difference between percentile ranks and percentiles. If our raw score of 60 has a percentile rank of 15, then the fifteenth percentile in our distribution is 60. In the same vein, if our raw score of 72 has a PR of 50, the 50th percentile or median of our distribution is 72. More specifically, fifteen percent of our scores lie below raw score 60 and 50 percent of our scores lie below raw score 72. A percentile rank is a numerical index that gives the percent of persons scoring below a specific point on the score scale. A percentile, on the other hand is a point or score in the distribution of scores indicating the percent of pupils falling below it. The formula for a percentile from group data is similar to the formulas for Q_1, Q_2, or Q_3 discussed previously.

Figure 12 also shows the percentile ranks for the 30 raw scores.

The relationship between the standard deviation, standard scores, and percentile ranks is presented in Figure 13. It shows the relatedness of these scales for reporting relative position in a normally distributed group. Close inspection of Figure 13, for example, suggests that a raw score one standard deviation above the mean (84 in our distribution) can be expressed as a Z-score of 1.00, a T-score of 60, or a percentile rank of 84.

OTHER STATISTICAL MEASURES

It was suggested at the beginning of this chapter that a teacher needed to be skilled in the use and interpretation of statistics and that one could obtain the following types of

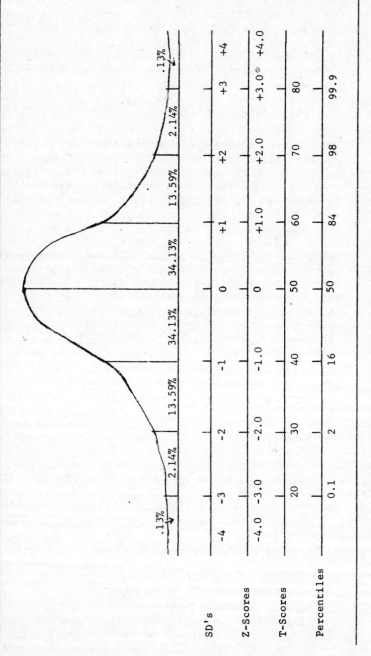

Figure 13. The Relationship Between the Standard Deviation, Standard Scores (Z-scores, T-scores), and Percentiles

information through a statistical analysis of data: (1)
typical performance of a group (central tendency); (2) how
the scores are dispersed around the central tendency (variability); (3) a clear portrayal of the score in graphic form
(frequency polygon, histogram); and (4) the transformation of
scores into a meaningful form (standard scores, percentiles).
These procedures were illustrated in the preceding section.
It was suggested, furthermore, that a knowledge of statistics
could provide information in terms of: (1) the relationship
of one variable to another; (2) the reliability of measurements; and (3) the validity of measurements. The statistical
technique used to establish the relationship between two
variables and the reliability and validity of measurements
is called correlation. The following section deals with the
statistical technique (meaning and computation) of correlation, while Chapter 4 deals with correlation as it relates
to establishing the reliability and validity of measurements.

CORRELATION

It is frequently necessary to ascertain the degree of
relationship that exists between sets of scores representing
two or more variables, or between sets of scores obtained for
other reasons. Correlation is a statistical technique used
for establishing the relationship of two sets of test scores.
We may, for example, wish to determine the relationship of our
30 pupils' IQ scores to their Biology test scores or the
relationship of their Science aptitude scores to the Biology
test scores.

Statistically, correlation is defined as the degree to
which the paired scores of two (or more) sets of scores tend
to vary together. The coefficient of correlation is the
numerical index used to describe the degree of relationship
that exists between the two sets of scores. These numerical
indices for the correlation coefficient range from +1.00,
through 0, to -1.00. The range for the coefficients of
correlation is, therefore, ±1.00. A correlation coefficient
of +1.00 indicates a perfect positive correlation. A coefficient of -1.00 describes a perfect negative correlation.
A coefficient of 0 (or near 0) indicates little or no relationship between the test scores. Figure 14 shows graphs of these
coefficients of correlation. These figures are known as
scattergrams. The points represent pairs of scores, one
score on test or variable X, the other score on test or
variable Y. Each point occurs where the two scores coincide.
A line, called a regression line is drawn through the points.
If all the points fall in a straight line, we have either a
perfect positive or a perfect negative coefficient of

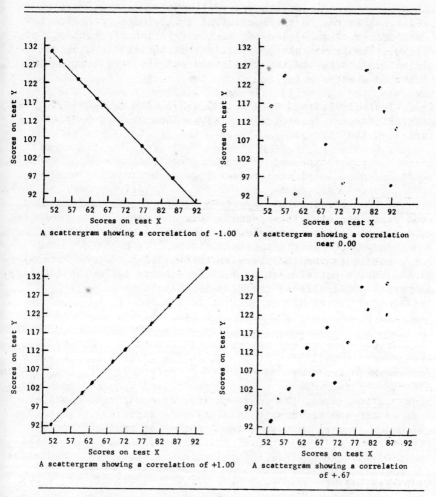

Figure 14. Graphs (Scattergrams) of Coefficients of Correlation

52

correlation. In a near 0 correlation, no straight line will pass through or near many of the points. Coefficients of correlation are rarely perfect.

The closer the coefficients are to +1.00 and -1.00 the greater the relationship between the pairs of test scores. The closer the relationships are to 0, the less relationship there is. A coefficient of -0.95 shows a higher degree of relationship than a coefficient of +0.78. A correlation coefficient of +0.45 shows a higher relationship than one of -0.20. The extent of the relationship between two variables is determined by the numerical value of the coefficient and not by its sign.

Table IV adapted from Dizney (1971, p. 76) provides some suggestions for interpreting the meanings or values of correlation coefficients.

Two major types of correlation coefficients are commonly used in educational measurement: Pearson Product-Moment Correlation and Spearman Rank-Order Correlation. Both of these correlation coefficients are interpreted in the same fashion and are therefore, interchangeable. The methods for computing the two coefficients of correlations are discussed below.

Let us assume that we wish to establish the statistical relationship between achievement in science and mental ability. In order to illustrate the relationship between these two variables, let us use our scores on the Biology test for our 30 pupils and their scores on a mental ability test (IQ or scholastic aptitude). The scores on the Biology test will be referred to as variable X, while the scores on the mental ability test will be referred to as the Y variable. Table V illustrates the computation of the two correlation coefficients Pearson Product-Moment Correlation (r) and Spearman Rank-Order Correlation (Rho). The former, (r), is considered a better method and is used more widely. The latter, (Rho), is used when one is dealing with a small number of pairs of scores (usually 20 or less). Both computations, nevertheless, will be used with an N of 30 pairs for the purpose of a comparative illustration. The practical application of these two coefficients will be discussed in Chapter IV which deals with the validity and reliability of measurements.

Our coefficient of .95 (Rho) or .96 (r) connotes a strong, direct relationship between our Biology test scores and the mental ability scores.

TABLE IV

GENERAL STATEMFNTS SUGGESTING THE MEANINGS
OF VARIOUS COEFFICIENTS OF CORRELATION

Values of r	Strength of Association
1.00	Perfect, positive
.80 to .99	Strong, direct
.60 to .79	Moderate, direct
.40 to .59	Slight, direct
.20 to .39	Weak but positive
-.20 to .20	Weak to chance
-.40 to -.21	Weak but negative
-.60 to -.41	Slight, inverse
-.80 to -.61	Moderate, inverse
-.99 to -.81	Strong, inverse
-1.00	Perfect, inverse

From H. Dizney, Classroom Evaluation for Teachers (Dubuque,
Iowa: William C. Brown Co., 1971). Used with permission.

TABLE V

COMPUTATION OF THE PEARSON PRODUCT-MOMENT AND
SPEARMAN RANK-ORDER CORRELATION COEFFICIENTS

Pearson's r

Pupil	Biology Test X	Mental Ability Test Y	XY
1	98	120	11760
2	94	115	10810
3	93	131	12183
4	89	125	11125
5	88	124	10912
6	84	104	8736
7	83	116	9628
8	82	112	9184
9	81	100	8100
10	79	109	8611
11	77	111	8547
12	76	103	7828
13	74	108	7992
14	74	99	7326
15	72	101	7272
16	71	98	6958
17	70	96	6720
18	70	95	6650
19	70	94	6580
20	69	104	7176
21	68	89	6052
22	66	91	6006
23	65	87	5655
24	64	86	5504
25	61	85	5185
26	60	82	4920
27	57	83	4731
28	55	84	4620
29	53	85	4505
30	50	81	4050
	$\Sigma X=2193$	$\Sigma Y=3018$	$\Sigma XY=225326$

$M_x = 73$ $M_y = 101$

$SD_x = 11$ $SD_y = 13$

$$r = \frac{\frac{\Sigma XY}{N} - M_x M_y}{(SD_x)(SD_y)} = \frac{7510.86 - 7373.00}{(11)(13)} = \frac{137.86}{143.00} = .96$$

$$r = .96$$

Spearman's Rho

Pupil	Biology Test X	Mental Ability Y	Rank x	Rank y	d	d^2
1	98	120	1	4	3	9
2	94	115	2	6	4	16
3	93	131	3	1	2	4
4	89	125	4	2	2	4
5	88	124	5	3	2	4
6	84	104	6	11.5	5.5	30.25
7	83	116	7	5	2	4
8	82	112	8	7	1	1
9	81	100	9	15	6	36
10	79	109	10	9	1	1
11	77	111	11	8	3	9
12	76	103	12	13	1	1
13	74	108	13.5	10	3.5	12.25
14	74	99	13.5	16	2.5	6.25
15	72	101	15	14	1	1
16	71	98	16	17	1	1
17	70	96	18	18	0	0
18	70	95	18	19	1	1
19	70	94	18	20	2	4
20	69	104	20	11.5	8.5	72.25
21	68	89	21	22	1	1
22	66	91	22	21	1	1
23	65	87	23	23	0	0
24	64	86	24	24	0	0
25	61	85	25	25.5	.5	.25
26	60	82	26	29	3	9
27	57	83	27	28	1	1
28	55	84	28	27	1	1
29	53	85	29	25.5	3.5	12.25
30	50	81	30	30	0	0
						$\Sigma d^2 = 242.5$

$$Rho = 1 - \frac{6 \Sigma d^2}{N(N^2-1)}$$

$$= 1 - \frac{1455}{26970}$$

$$= 1 - .05$$

$$= .95$$

$\Sigma =$ sum of

$d =$ difference between the pupil's rank on test X and that on test Y.

$N = $ # of pairs of scores

55

FORMULAS FOR THE VARIOUS MEASURES OF CENTRAL TENDENCY AND VARIABILITY

Formulas For Computations From Ungrouped Data

1. **Mean**

$$M = \frac{\Sigma X}{N}$$

M = Mean
Σ = "sum of"
N = Number of Scores

Formulas For Computations From Grouped Data

1. **Mean**

$$M = \frac{\Sigma fX'}{N}$$

M = Mean
Σ = "sum of"
f = frequencies
X'= Midpoints of class intervals
$\Sigma fX'$ = the sum of the frequencies in the class intervals times (X) the midpoints of the class intervals
N = Number of Scores

2. **Median**

$$Mdn = \left(\frac{N+1}{2}\right) \begin{array}{l} \text{Result count} \\ \text{up} \end{array}$$

N = Number of Scores

2. **Median**

$$Mdn = 1 + \left[\frac{N/2-F}{fm}\right]i$$

Mdn = Median
1 = Actual lower limit of class interval wherein the Mdn lies
N/2 = one-half the number of scores
F = The sum of the frequencies of all class intervals below 1
fm = frequency of scores within interval containing Mdn
i = Size of the class interval

3. **Mode**

Mo = Most frequent score
Mo = Mode

3. **Mode**

Mo = Midpoint of the class interval having the highest frequency (f)

4. Range

$R = H-L$
R = Range
H = Highest Score
L = Lowest Score

5. Quartile Deviation

$$Q = \frac{Q_3 - Q_1}{2}$$

Q = Quartile Deviation
Q_3 = 3rd Quartile
Q_1 = 1st Quartile

3rd Quartile

Q_3 = 3/4N Result count
        up
Q_3 = 3rd Quartile
N = Number of Scores

1st Quartile

Q_1 = 1/4N Result count
        up
Q_1 = 1st Quartile
N = Number of Scores

4. Range

$R = H-L$
R = Range
H = Highest Score
L = Lowest Score

5. Quartile Deviation

$$Q = \frac{Q_3 - Q_1}{2}$$

Q = Quartile Deviation
Q_3 = 3rd Quartile
Q_1 = 1st Quartile

3rd Quartile - 1st Quartile

$$Q_3 = 1 + \frac{3N/4 - \text{cum } f}{f_q} i$$

$$Q_1 = 1 + \frac{N/4 - \text{cum } f}{f_q} i$$

Q_3 = 3rd Quartile
Q_1 = 1st Quartile
1 = actual lower limit of
      class interval wherein
      quartile lies
cum f = the sum f the fre-
           quencies of all
           class intervals
           below
f_q = frequency of scores
        within the class inter-
        vals where the quartiles
        lie
i = size of the class
      interval

6a. Standard Deviation

$$SD = \sqrt{\frac{\Sigma X^2}{N} - M^2}$$

SD = Standard Deviation

$\sqrt{}$ = Square root
ΣX^2 = Sum of "squared"
             raw scores
N = Number of Scores
M^2 = Squared mean

6. Standard Deviation

$$SD = \sqrt{\frac{\Sigma f x^2}{N}}$$

SD = Standard Deviation

$\sqrt{}$ = Square root
Σ = "sum of"
f = frequencies
x = X'-M (Midpoint of C.I.-
      Mean)

6. **Standard Deviation (cont'd.)**

Σfx^2 = the sum of the class intervals times (X) the squared differences between midpoints of the class intervals and the mean of the distribution.

6b. **Standard Deviation**

$$SD = \frac{\Sigma \text{ highest } 1/6 - \Sigma \text{ lowest } 1/6}{1/2N}$$

SD = Standard Deviation
Σ highest 1/6 = the sum of the highest 1/6 of the scores
Σ lowest 1/6 = the sum of the lowest 1/6 of the scores
N = Number of Scores

Chapter IV

VALIDITY, RELIABILITY, AND USABILITY: DESIRABLE
CHARACTERISTICS OF EDUCATIONAL MEASUREMENTS

Measurement devices (i.e., teacher-made tests, standardized tests, etc.), though varied in type and purpose, should possess certain minimal characteristics. A good measuring instrument measures what it is supposed to measure to a high degree, consistently, and with a minimum expenditure of time, energy, and money (Lien, 1971). This definition of a measuring instrument includes the major desirable characteristics of: validity (the extent to which an instrument measures what it is supposed to measure), reliability (the consistency of a measuring instrument), and usability (the adequacy of an instrument in terms of a minimum of time, energy, and money). This chapter deals with these three characteristics.

VALIDITY

Most references on the term validity define it as: the extent or the degree to which an instrument measures what it purports to measure. This is acceptable as a relatively general or generic definition of the term. The crucial issue with respect to validity, however, is in terms of the specific purposes for which different instruments are designed. Validity should thus be defined at various levels and in various ways. The flavor of the concept can be conveyed by the types of questions that an analysis of validity seeks to answer: Valid for what? How well does the test do the job it is employed to do? What traits are being measured by the test? Is the test actually measuring what it was designed to measure? What can be predicted from the test scores? Validity information, then, indicates the degree to which the test is capable of achieving certain aims. Tests are used for several types of judgments, and for each type of judgment, a different type of investigation is required to establish validity (French and Michael, 1966). Basically, then, validity is always concerned with the specific use to be made of the results and with the truthfulness of proposed interpretations.

When the term validity is to be used, in relation to testing and evaluation, there are a number of cautions to be borne in mind (Gronlund, 1971):

1. Validity pertains to the results of a test, or evaluation instrument, and not to the instrument

itself. We sometimes speak of the validity of a
test, for the sake of convenience, but it is more
appropriate to speak of the validity of the test
results, or more specifically, of the validity of
the interpretation to be made from the results.

2. Validity is a matter of degree. It does not exist
    on an all-or-none basis. Consequently, we should
    avoid thinking of evaluation results as valid or
    invalid. Validity is best considered in terms of
    categories that specify degree, such as high
    validity, moderate validity, and low validity.

3. Validity is always specific to some particular use.
    It should never be considered a general quality.
    For example, the results of an arithmetic test may
    have a high degree of validity for indicating
    computational skill, a low degree of validity for
    indicating arithmetical reasoning, a moderate degree
    of validity for predicting success in future
    mathematics courses, and no validity for predicting
    success in art or music. Thus, when appraising or
    describing validity, it is necessary to consider the
    use to be made of the results. Evaluation results
    are never just valid; they have a different degree
    of validity for each particular use to which they
    are put. (p. 77)

Five major types of validity have been defined and are
now commonly used in educational measurement. These include:
face validity, content validity, predictive validity, concurrent validity, and construct validity. Predictive and
concurrent validity are subsumed under the common name,
criterion-related validity. Although the primary interest
of the classroom teacher is probably in face and content
validity, he should, nevertheless, be familiar with the other
types which are typically used in evaluating and using standardized tests.

Face Validity

Face validity is frequently confused with content
validity. While this type of validity is classified as
neither technically logical nor empirical in nature, it is
nevertheless a factor which is capable of influencing the
validity of a test. Face validity applies more to whether
a test appears to measure relevant information and content.
When a teacher-made final examination is to be used, for
example, it is important that the pupils feel that the test is

appropriate in vocabulary and content in that it stresses what they have studied. Face validity may be of minimal importance in some tests and of maximal importance in others because it affects the attitude of the pupils toward the test.

Content Validity

Content validity, sometimes referred to as curricular validity, is the type of validity deemed most relevant and useful to the classroom teacher. The major characteristics of content validity are:

1. It is most appropriately used in connection with achievement testing.

2. An achievement test has content validity if it represents faithfully the objectives of a given instructional sequence and reflects the emphasis accorded these objectives.

3. It is most often determined on the basis of expert judgment, rather than on a statistical or empirical basis.

4. It is based on an examination of an outline of the content and objectives of the unit for which the test was designed.

5. Its aim in testing is to estimate how a person would perform, at present, in a defined "universe" of situations, of which the test constitutes a sample.

6. It is assessed, as indicated above, on a logical analysis of the relationship between the content and abilities that a test is supposed to cover and the actual content of the test items.

Predictive Validity

This type of validity is considered when one wishes to use a test for predicting the future status of individuals. Predictive validity is characterized as follows:

1. In order to determine the predictive validity of an instrument, it is necessary to establish an external criterion against which one's predictions can be compared.

2. It is usually possible to express predictive validity in terms of the correlation coefficient (validity coefficient) between the predicted status and the criterion.

3. The criterion against which the test is correlated to insure predictive validity should be related to the test, should be reliable, and should be practical.

4. Its aim in testing is to predict a person's <u>future</u> on the test or on some external variable.

Concurrent Validity

Concurrent validity is frequently referred to as status validity. It is used to determine how well a test can obtain more easily, quickly, and inexpensively estimates of the examinee's present status with respect to some attribute that cannot feasibly be measured by a more direct method. The major characteristics of concurrent validity are:

1. It is always expressed in terms of the relationship between the test and an accepted <u>contemporary</u> (administered at about the same time) criterion.

2. The correlation coefficient provides a quantitative measure of this relationship, thereby making it an empirically derived type of validity.

3. The external criterion used for concurrent validity must be related, reliable, and practical.

4. Its aim in testing is to estimate a person's <u>present</u> status with respect to some attribute external to the test.

Construct Validity

Construct validity concerns the extent to which a test tells us something about a meaningful characteristic of the individual. Major characteristics of this type of validity include:

1. Evidence of construct validity is used to determine the trait or characteristic measured by the test.

2. Evidence of construct validity may be provided by (a) its correlations with other tests, particularly those which are accepted measures of the same

construct; (b) its correlations with other characteristics of the individual, e.g., attitudes, personality; and (c) its correlations with factors in the individual's environment which would be expected to affect test performance.

3. Its aim in testing is to make inferences concerning the degree to which a person possesses a trait or construct, presumably reflected in the test performance.

In the interest of utility, comprehension, and summarization, we may indicate the different types of validity in Table VI which represents a composite from various sources (Brown, 1970; French and Michael, 1966; Tiedeman, 1972; and Storey, 1970).

Numerous factors tend to make test results invalid for their intended purpose. Some factors which the teacher should be alerted to, whether constructing classroom tests or selecting standardized tests have been listed by Gronlund (1971):

1. Unclear directions. Directions which do not clearly indicate to the pupil how to respond to the items, whether it is permissible to guess, and how to record the answers will tend to reduce validity.

2. Reading vocabulary and sentence structure too difficult. Vocabulary and sentence structure which is too complicated for the pupils taking the test will result in the test measuring reading comprehension and aspects of intelligence rather than the aspects of pupil behavior that the test is intended to measure.

3. Inappropriate level of difficulty of the test items. Items which are too easy or too difficult will not provide reliable discriminations among pupils and will therefore lower validity.

4. Poorly constructed test items. Test items which unintentionally provide clues to the answer will tend to measure the pupils' alertness in detecting clues as well as the aspects of pupil behavior that the test is intended to measure.

5. Ambiguity. Ambiguous statements in test items contribute to misinterpretations and confusion. Ambiguity

63

TABLE VI

FIVE MAJOR TYPES OF VALIDITY AND THEIR CHARACTERISTICS

Kinds of Validity	Question Asked	How Demonstrated or Evaluated	Process Involved in Demonstration	Examples
1. Face	How appropriate do the vocabulary and content used in the test seem to the examinee?	Logically-	The examinee, upon examining the test content, does not consider it absurd	A test in elementary school arithmetic should have vocabulary and content which pertains to the elementary school child
2. Content or Curricular	How would the individual perform in the universe of situations of which the test items are sample?	Logically-by expert opinion estimating the adequacy of sampling	Expert examines the content or curriculum to be measured, examines test items, and judges the degree to which they correspond	A teacher-made test sampling or testing the content of a given unit of the course
3. Predictive	How well do the scores on the test predict of forecast an individual's future standing on some variable of particular significance that is different from the test?	Empirically-statistically	Administer test, wait months or years, obtain scores on the behavior to be predicted, and correlated the two sets of scores	Using a mental ability test to predict elementary or high school grades

TABLE VI (CONTINUED)

Kinds of Validity	Question Asked	How Demonstrated or Evaluated	Process Involved in Demonstration	Examples
4. Concurrent	How well do the scores on the test estimate an individual's present standing on some variable of particular significance that is different from the test?	Empirically-statistically	Administer one test, administer a second test within hours or days, and correlate the two sets of scores	Comparing the results obtained on a mental ability test with those obtained on an achievement test
5. Construct	What trait does the test measure?	Empirically and by expert opinion	Expert examines construct in relation to the test items designed to measure it and judges the degree of relationship. Test scores may be correlated with scores believed to represent the construct.	Developing a test to define a trait such as intelligence or creativity

sometimes confuses the better pupils more than the poorer pupils, causing the items to discriminate in a negative direction.

6. <u>Test items inappropriate for the outcomes being measured</u>. Attempting to measure understandings, thinking skills, and other complex types of achievement with test forms that are appropriate only for measuring factual knowledge will invalidate the results.

7. <u>Test too short</u>. A test is only a sample of the many questions that might be asked. If a test is too short to provide a representative sample of the behavior we are interested in, validity will suffer accordingly.

8. <u>Improper arrangement of items</u>. Test items are typically arranged in order of difficulty with the easiest items first. Placing difficult items early in the test may cause pupils to spend too much time on these and prevent them from reaching items they could easily answer. Improper arrangement may also influence validity by having a detrimental effect on pupil motivation.

9. <u>Identifiable pattern of answers</u>. Placing answers in some systematic pattern (e.g., T, T, F, F, or A, B, C, D) will enable students to guess the answers to some items more easily and this will lower validity. (pp. 93-94)

In relation to the above-mentioned factors which tend to invalidate a test, Lien (1971) suggests some principles that will help the classroom teacher prepare instruments which are more valid:

1. Make a plan for the construction and use of the measuring device. This includes:
   Listing the specific objectives for which the device is to be used. Listing the main ideas of content or traits which will show growth toward the objectives. Stating the value of the device in relation to other devices to be used (this is a percentage based on 100% for all of the devices to be used).

2. Follow this plan in constructing the device so that the end produce will reflect the original "blueprint."

3. Construct the devices when the unit is being planned and/or being taught.

4. Be sure that the format of the device includes all of the things which the student needs to know to proceed effectively in using the instrument (such as clear and complete directions, clear samples, clear answering system, and the like).

5. Specific principles for the construction of good tests are:
   (a) Be sure that the items are of the proper degree of difficulty for the grade level.
   (b) Be sure that the items proceed from easier to more difficult.
   (c) Be sure that the items are worded properly and that appropriate vocabulary and grammar are used.
   (d) Be sure that there are no items which will be answered by all or failed by all. There is one exception to this rule. Usually the first item or so, depending on the length of the test, is so easy that all can answer it correctly. This is known before the test is administered. The purpose of this type of item is for motivational purposes only - that is, to get the student started on the test with some feeling of self-confidence.
   (e) Be sure that no trick or catch questions are used.
   (f) Be sure to have full and complete directions for each type of item.
   (g) Be sure to make generous use of samples, especially in new types of items.
   (h) Be sure that the test is long enough to measure what it is supposed to measure.
   (i) Be sure that the individual items differentiated between the good and poor pupils in the class. To determine this, one can make an item analysis. (pp. 48-49)

RELIABILITY

Reliability is defined as the extent to which a test measures consistently what it purports to measure. Like validity, reliability is a necessary though not a sufficient indication of the adequacy of a test. The meaning of reliability, as applied to testing and evaluation, can be clarified by noting the following general points (Gronlund, 1971):

1. Reliability refers to the <u>results</u> obtained with an
    evaluation instrument and not to the instrument it-
    self. Any particular instrument may have a number
    of different reliabilities, depending on the group
    involved and the situation in which it is used. Thus,
    it is more appropriate to speak of the reliability of
    "the test scores," or of "the measurement," than of
    "the test," or "the instrument."

2. A closely related point is that an estimate of
    reliability always refers to a particular type of
    consistency. Test scores are not reliable in
    general. They are reliable (or able to be genera-
    lized) over different periods of time, over different
    samples of questions, over different raters, and the
    like. It is possible for test scores to be consis-
    tent in one of these respects and not in another.
    The appropriate type of consistency in a particular
    case is dictated by the use to be made of the results.
    For example, if we wish to know what individuals will
    be like at some future time, constancy of scores is
    highly important. On the other hand, if we want to
    measure an individual's shifts in anxiety from
    moment to moment, we shall need a measure which lacks
    constancy over occasions in order to obtain the
    information we desire. Thus, for different inter-
    pretations we need different analyses of consistency.
    Treating reliability as a general characteristic can
    lead to erroneous interpretations.

3. Reliability is a necessary but not a sufficient
    condition for validity. A test which provides
    totally inconsistent results cannot possible pro-
    vide truthful information about the behavior being
    measured. On the other hand, highly consistent
    test results may be measuring the wrong thing or may
    be used in ways that are inappropriate. Thus, low
    reliability can be expected to restrict the degree of
    validity that is obtained, but high reliability
    provides no assurance that a satisfactory degree of
    validity will be present. In short, <u>reliability</u>
    <u>merely</u> <u>provides</u> <u>the</u> <u>consistency</u> <u>which</u> <u>makes</u> <u>validity</u>
    <u>possible</u>.
        Although a highly reliable measure may have
    little or no validity, a measure which has been shown
    to have a satisfactory degree of predictive validity
    must of necessity possess sufficient reliability.
    Thus, where we are interested only in predicting a
    specific criterion, reliability will be of little

concern if predictive validity is satisfactory.

4. Unlike validity, reliability is strictly a statistical concept. Logical analysis of a test will provide little evidence concerning the reliability of the scores. The test must be administered, one or more times, to an appropriate group of persons and the consistency of the results determined. This consistency may be expressed in terms of shifts in the relative standing of persons in the group or in terms of the amount of variation to be expected in a specific individual's score. Consistency of the first type is reported by means of a correlation coefficient called a reliability coefficient. Consistency of the second type is reported by means of the standard error of measurement. Both methods of expressing reliability are widely used and should be understood by persons responsible for interpreting test results. (pp. 101-102)

Just as there are several ways of operationalizing or defining validity, there are several ways to operationalize reliability. The types or definitions of reliability are based on the consistency of the scores obtained by the examinees in a given population when two distributions of scores for them are obtained. Consistency of performance, and thus reliability, may be expressed in terms of the correlation between performance of pupils on successive administrations of the same measure. The correlation coefficient used to determine reliability is calculated and interpreted in the same manner as that used in computing statistical estimates of validity. The only difference between a validity coefficient and a reliability coefficient is that the former is based on the relationship with an outside criterion (something outside the test itself), while the latter is based on agreement between two sets of results from the same procedure or test.

Four major types of reliability are common in current educational measurement. These include: test-retest, equivalence, test-retest with equivalence; and internal consistency. The two methods most commonly used by the classroom teacher are test-retest and internal consistency. All methods, however, will be discussed since standardized tests make use of these methods and teachers should be familiar with them.

Test-Retest Reliability

Test-retest reliability, also referred to as stability reliability, is a measure of the extent to which test scores are stable over a specified time period. In order to determine this type of reliability, pupils are administered the same test twice and the scores are correlated using the Pearson's Product-Moment Correlation technique or Spearman's Rho. If the test is reliable or stable, pupils will tend to retain the same ordinal positions when the results of the two sets are scored and examined. More specifically, those pupils obtaining high scores on the first administration will tend to have high scores on the second administration; those students with low scores on the first administration will also tend to have low scores on the second administration.

Equivalence Reliability

This type of reliability involves the administration of one form of a test to pupils followed in close succession by the administration of a second test which is different but equivalent or parallel to the first test. Equivalence refers to the fact that the two tests should be the same in terms of content, validity, item difficulty, etc. Following the administration of the two tests to the same group of pupils, the resulting test scores are correlated thus providing a correlation coefficient which indicates whether the two forms are equivalent.

Test-Retest With Equivalence Reliability

This type of reliability is a combination of the two previously discussed types of reliability. This method of estimating reliability involves the administration of one form of a test followed by the administration of an equivalent form after an interval of time has elapsed. The results of the two test administrations are then correlated and the obtained correlation coefficient indicates the reliability of the scores.

Internal Consistency Reliability

There are times when the procedures for estimating reliability which were previously discussed are not feasible nor practical. It is possible, therefore, to estimate the reliability of test scores by simply administering the test once, dividing the test into two parts or halves and then correlating the two halves of the test. To divide or split into two halves, one should take the even-numbered items as the other half. This procedure will provide two scores for each pupil which are then correlated, thus providing a measure of internal consistency. This reliability coefficient provides an indication of the extent to which the two halves of the test are consistent. The reliability coefficient determined through the internal consistency or split-half procedure described above represents the correlation between two halves of a test. In order to determine the reliability of the full test, it is necessary to apply a formula to correct for the fact that the original reliability coefficient was based on two halves. The Spearman-Brown formula is usually applied to correct for this. For use in the split-half procedure, this formula is as follows:

$$r = \frac{2(r_s)}{1 + r_s}$$

Where r = reliability on the full test

r_s = the reliability coefficient obtained using the two halves of the original test

To illustrate the use of the formula, let us assume that the coefficient of internal consistency via the split-half method or between the two halves of the test is .75.

$$r = \frac{2(.75)}{1 = .75} = \frac{1.50}{1.75} = .86$$

Another practical method for estimating the internal consistency reliability of a test is through the use of Diederich's (1964) modification of the Kuder-Richard Fromula 21. This formula is as follows:

$$r = 1 - \frac{M(k-M)}{Ks^2}$$

Where r = the reliability coefficient
M = the mean of the test scores
K = the number of items in the test
s = the standard deviation of the test

To illustrate the use of this formula, let us use the descriptive data obtained in a previous chapter using the 100-item Biology test:

$$M = 73$$
$$s = 11$$
$$K = 100$$
$$r = 1 - \frac{73(100-73)}{100(11)^2}$$
$$= .84$$

Again, in the interest of utility, comprehension, and summarization, the various types of reliability are presented in Table VII which represents a composite from several sources (Storey, 1970; Gronlund, 1971; Dizney, 1971; and Lindeman, 1967).

A number of factors which affect reliability have been listed by Lien (1971):

1. General factors
   Length of the instrument - Generally, the longer the instrument, the greater is the reliability.

2. Teacher factors
   Classroom Environment - Generally, the better the classroom environment, the greater is the reliability.
   Motivation - The more positive the motivation, the greater is the reliability.
   Directions - The more consistent and complete the directions, the greater is the reliability.
   Supervision - The better the supervision, the more reliable is the instrument.

3. Pupil factors
   Physical Condition - The better the condition of the student physically, the more reliable, generally, are the results.
   Emotional Condition - The more stable the pupil, the more stable, generally, are the results.
   Desire to Learn - Generally, the greater the motivation of a pupil, the more consistent are the results.
   (p. 51)

Storey (1970) suggests that the test maker can provide for reliability by:

1. Insuring that his test is of sufficient length (from 30 to 50 multiple-choice items, or from one-half to three-quarters of an hour of testing time) to adequately sample the behavior to be assessed.

72

TABLE VII

SUMMARY OF TYPES OF RELIABILITY COEFFICIENTS, PROCEDURE
FOR OBTAINING ADVANTAGES AND DISADVANTAGES

Types of Reliability	Procedure for Obtaining	Advantages	Disadvantages
Test-retest (stability)	The same test is administered on two occasions to the same pupils.	Assures complete equivalence in test content. Good when element of speed is emphasized in a test.	Practice effect; memory for answers given; change in phenomena measured from one time to the next. Impractical for the teacher.
Equivalence (parallel)	Two forms of the same test are administered to the same group in close succession.	Removes problem of selecting a proper time interval between administrations.	May not have true parallel form of test. It is more difficult to construct two forms of a test than just one.
Test-retest with Equivalence (stability-equivalence)	Two forms of the same test are administered to the same group on two different occasions with a longer time interval between administrations.	Minimizes practice or memory effects, provides more accurate estimate of reliability because the estimate is based on a larger sampling of test items.	Difficult to decide on an appropriate time interval between test administration.
Internal Consistency (split-half, or Kuder-Richardson)	The test is administered once; two halves of the test correlated them corrected for length. Also one can score total test and apply K-R formula.	Easiest and most practical to use insofar as the classroom teacher is concerned.	Impractical to use with tests where speed is the prime factor.

2. Using homogeneous item types clustered around the essentials of the content.

3. Attempting to set all items within the middle range of difficulty (difficulty indexes of between .40 and .60).

4. Endeavoring to set items that will discriminate adequately between the better and the poorer students.

5. Tending toward speed rather than power tests in order to minimize the changing of responses for no better reason than that the student has time on his hands in which to make such changes.

6. Testing for reliability over the widest range of talent for which the test is designed.

7. Editing items carefully before using them to insure that both the language used and the task set are clear and specific. (p. 35)

USABILITY

Usability, a third and major characteristic of effective tests or instruments, consists of a number of factors which make it convenient to administer and use. The following factors are considered in determining the usability of an instrument (Green, 1970):

1. Administrability. Standardized tests are frequently administered by the classroom teacher, who may have little formal background in measurement; therefore, the instructions for administration of a test need to be followed to the letter to preserve the test standardization. The better tests contain very specific instructions for the person administering the test and for the student taking the test. Furthermore, sample exercises are provided at the beginning of the test, or sub-tests if the items change, to insure understanding and to establish desirable test psychology. Since the exact words needed to administer the test are printed in the test manuals, they should be read verbatim, and individual help should not be given students except where the instructions permit it.

2. Scorability. The scoring of achievement tests is often done by school personnel, although most of the

tests now have provisions for machine scoring. Machine scoring is feasible if the cost is low and the scoring machine is convenient to expedite scoring. When tests are machine scored, the answer sheets should be returned so that the teacher can detect any problem situations, such as an individual's misunderstandings.

3. Economy. Tests should be reasonably economical, although this is not always the primary consideration. An original high cost for test booklets which can be used several years with separate answer sheets may, in the long run, be more economical than cheaper booklets which cannot be reused. Likewise, cheaper cost is undesirable if considerable quality is sacrificed.

4. Format. Format of the test is also important. The test should be printed in large, clear print on good quality paper. If the booklet is to be reused with answer sheets, the quality of its physical construction should be such that it can be reused several times. In this case, also, the pages should be arranged so that the answer sheet can be conveniently fitted into the test booklet with little possibility of error in matching booklet and answer sheet.

5. Norms. The norms on the test should be comparable to those on the other tests used in the school. Otherwise meaningful summaries or profiles of a pupil's test record are difficult to make. Many tests now have several methods of reporting scores, e.g., grade norms, percentile rank, T-scores, and several standard scores based on standard deviation. (pp. 81-84)

Green (1963) suggests that the usability of a teacher-made test can be assured by observing the following rules:

1. Have the test typed and duplicated so that each pupil will have a copy. The copies of the test should have large, clear print on good-quality paper, and the stencils should always be proofread before the tests are duplicated.

2. Directions to the pupil should accompany each part of the test. These directions hould be explicit in indicating the mode of response and should be simple enough for all to understand.

3. <u>The test should be designed to fit the time limits of the class period</u>. Teachers frequently make tests either too long or too short. The test which is too long frustrates the pupil; the test which is too short may give inadequate sampling of learning.

4. <u>The test should be set up so that it can be readily scored</u>. In the upper grades and the secondary school, answer sheets may be used, and prepared keys or scoring stencils will facilitate the scoring of most tests.

5. <u>Care should be exercised in planning the test to make it economical in terms of time required for test construction, duplication, and scoring</u>. Teaching requires a great deal of time; and although the evaluation of learning is an essential element in good teaching, it should not become so burdensome as to usurp necessary lesson-planning time.

6. <u>Norms of pupil performance should be established from test results</u>. Teachers who have kept records of the performances of their previous classes on specific tests or test items have a scale against which to compare the performance of their current classes. Such comparisons are much preferable to the subjective judgment of the teacher in determining the quality of a class's test performance. (pp. 98-99)

Chapter V

THE TEACHER-MADE TEST: CONSTRUCTION AND SCORING

The most frequently used method or technique for measuring
and evaluating pupil progress by the classroom teacher is the
teacher-made test. This type of test may involve true-false,
multiple-choice, essay exams, etc. Yet it is quite common to
find teachers who have had no specific training in the use and
construction of these types of tests. Such teachers often
design tests on a trial and error basis. Similarly, many
teachers design such tests with little thought of the relationship between what these tests measure and the instructional
objectives. Because the examinations emphasize trivial points
which had been either neglected in class or given only cursory
consideration, the teacher has little notion of the effectiveness of his instructional objectives. For this teacher, tests
may become a series of puzzles designed to fool the student
instead of instruments for measuring the relative attainment
of classroom objectives and pupil progress.

This chapter will, therefore, attempt to focus on the
teacher-made test with respect to: (1) the relationship
between educational objectives and the teacher-made test; (2)
planning the teacher-made test; and (3) types of test items
including short-answer items, true-false items, multiple-
choice items, matching items, essay items and oral examinations.

EDUCATIONAL OBJECTIVES

The first and most important step in planning a teacher-
made test is to define the educational objectives or the objectives of instruction. Although a teacher may have access to
curriculum guides, the taxonomies of educational objectives
developed by Bloom (1956) and Krathwohl (1964) and texts on
the development of educational objectives by Plowman (1971)
and Kibler, Barker, and Miles (1970), the ultimate responsibility for selecting objectives suitable for the group of
students that he is teaching and stating the objectives in
such a way that they can guide instruction and the evaluation
of pupil progress rests with the teacher. In this book, the
assumption is made that the pre-service or in-service teacher
has had previous training in how to define and construct
educational objectives. If this is not the case, the afore-
mentioned sources should be consulted. As a review, however,
the author suggests that the teacher examine the following
characteristics that a set of instructional objectives should
possess:

1. Objectives should be stated in terms of student behavior, not in terms of learning activities or purposes of the teacher. For example, "Observes bacteria through a microscope" is not a satisfactory statement of an objective. This describes a learning activity. Why does a teacher want the students to observe bacteria? An analysis of the activities and contents of the course of study in which the objective appears indicates that the teacher wants the student to know the characteristics of organisms that cause diseases, and that observation of bacteria is incidental to this objective. It would be better to state the objective as, "Recalls characteristics of organisms that cause diseases."

2. Objectives should begin with an active verb that indicates the behavior that a student should show in dealing with content. This format tends to guarantee a focus on the student and what he does. The objective should not consist of a list of content. For example, the statement "Scurvy, beriberi, rickets, and pellagra are caused by a lack of vitamins in the body" is a statement of content not a statement of an objective. The objective should be stated, "Identifies certain disease conditions that are caused by lack of vitamins."

3. Objectives should be stated in terms of observable changes in student behavior. For example, an objective formulated as, "Always practices good health habits to prevent the spread of disease? is not stated in observable terms. The inclusion of "always" in the formulation means that it is impossible to gather the evidence needed to judge the achievement of the students. One cannot always observe a student. Another example is the statement, "Does his share to create good emotional atmosphere during meals at home." The behavior specified in this statement occurs in a situation outside of school in which the teacher would be unable to observe the student. It is unlikely that he is going to be able to get relevant evidence on the achievement of the objective. Another example is the statement, "Feels secure in making wise choices of food." In this statement, "feels secure" is unobservable; it is a covert characteristic of a student. One cannot observe a feeling of security. One can only observe behavior and perhaps make inferences about the security of the student.

78

4. Objectives should be stated precisely using terms that have uniform meaning. For example, in the objective, "Understands the responsibility of the community in control of communicable disease" the word "understands" means different things to different people. To one teacher it may mean that the students can name the different agencies in the community that have responsibility for controlling communicable disease. To another it may mean that the student, given a novel problem concerning communicable disease, can identify the appropriate community agency or agencies and indicate the services or actions to be expected from these agencies.

5. Objectives should be unitary; each statement should relate to only one process. For instance, the objective, "Knows elementary principles of immunization and accepts immunization willingly," contains two processes, a cognitive process of recall of information and an affective process of acceptance of an action. The two processes are quite different and require different evaluative procedures to obtain relevant evidence on their achievement. If both are important instructional objectives, then they should be stated as two separate objectives.

6. Objectives should be stated at an appropriate level of generality. On the one hand, the statement of an objective should not be so general and global as to be meaningless nor on the other hand should the statements be so narrow and specific that the educational process seems to be made up of isolated bits and pieces. In the latter case, an adequate list of objectives becomes too long and too unwieldy to use effectively. For example, the objective, "Knows nutrition" is too vague to serve any useful purpose. On the other hand, a series of statements such as "Identifies the function of proteins in the body," "Identifies the function of fats in the body," "Identifies the function of carbohydrates in the body," "Identifies the function of vitamins in the body," not only becomes boring to read but is also unnecessarily specific. At an appropriate level of generality, all the specific statements could be combined into one statement that reads, "Identifies the function of the five classes of nutrients in the body."

7. Objectives should represent intended direct outcomes
of a planned series of learning experiences. For
example, it is obvious that one would never write
as an educational objective for eighth graders
"Increases in height" simply because health instruction is not directed toward making eighth graders
taller. However, it is common to find statements of
objectives that deal with attitudes in programs in
which no particular instructional effort is given
to the development of attitudes.

8. Objectives should be realistic in terms of the time
available for teaching and the characteristics of the
students. An example of an unrealistic objective
would be, "Understands the reasons why people become drug addicts." This is unrealistic simply
because no one knows why people become drug addicts;
therefore it is impossible to teach toward this objective. (Thorndike and Hagen, 1969, pp. 35-37)

PLANNING THE TEST

As mentioned previously, the first and most important
step in planning a test is to define the educational objectives.
Other steps in planning the test are: (1) specifications of
the content to be covered, and (2) preparing the test blueprint
or table of specifications. The content and a statement of
process objectives represent the two dimensions into which a
test plan should be fitted. These two dimensions need to be
put together to see which objectives especially relate to
which segments of content and to provide a complete framework
for the development of the test (Thorndike and Hagen, 1969).

The necessity of writing clear and explicit instructional
objectives has been previously emphasized. It will, of course,
aid test construction very little for the teacher to formulate
clear, specific objectives and then not use them. One of
the most efficient ways to utilize well-written objectives in
test construction is by means of a test blueprint or table of
specifications. A table of specifications is essentially a
two-way grid, with the content outlined along the vertical
axis and the expected behavioral changes along the horizontal
axis. These two axes, however, are frequently reversed. Several advantages may result from the proper use of a table of
specifications, the more important of which are suggested by
Smith and Adams (1966):

1. It enables the teacher to build content validity into
    his tests. If the test items are classified in a
    table of specifications as they are written, the
    teacher can easily see if he is neglecting a signifi-
    cant objective or overemphasizing a minor one.

2. It enables the teacher to have a clearer perspective
    of a unit of work and the specific behavioral changes
    he hopes to bring about through it. This more pre-
    cise picture enables him to do a more efficient job
    of both teaching and testing.

3. It is of diagnostic value for both teacher and student
    If the test items have been classified in a table of
    specifications, the student can determine the parti-
    cular content areas and behaviors in which he is
    having difficulty. In the same way, the teacher can
    check on his own effectiveness by noting areas and
    objectives in which substantial numbers of the class
    are having difficulty.

The table of specifications is the blueprint, then, from
which a type of test may be selected and actual test construction may proceed. However, at this point it may be appropriate
to enumerate several principles of general test construction
which should be followed to insure a high-quality measuring
instrument which are suggested by Green (1963):

1. The test should be long enough to be valid and reliabl
    but short enough to be usable.

2. A measurement test should be a power test, wherein the
    first few items are simple enough for all students to
    answer.

3. The test should be designed in such a way that reading
    rate and comprehension do not unduly influence the
    test scores.

4. A test should generally consist of no more than two
    or three types of items, and all the items of one
    type should be included in one section.

5. The test items should be clear and concise, without
    the confusion of unnecessary words or unusual vocabu-
    lary.

6. The test directions should be clear and explicit.

7. The test items should have a simple method of indicating responses, and they should be easy to score.

8. The test should be typed and reproduced by ditto or mimeograph so that each pupil can have a copy.

9. The test should be appropriate to the ability and age level of the pupils.

TYPES OF TEST ITEMS

This section will emphasize the various test-item forms including short-answer items, true-false items, multiple-choice items, matching items, essay items, and oral examinations. Short-answer, true-false, multiple-choice, and matching items are typically referred to as <u>objective</u> tests, while essay and oral examinations are usually referred to as <u>subjective</u> examinations. Ebel (1965, pp. 84-109) has described the following differences and similarities of objective and essay tests:

Differences

Objective tests	Essay tests
1. Requires student to choose among two or more alternatives.	1. Requires the student to plan his own answer and express it in his own words.
2. Consists of many rather specific questions requiring only brief answers.	2. Consists of relatively few, more general questions which call for extended answers.
3. Students spend most of their time reading and thinking.	3. Students spend most of their time in thinking and writing.
4. Quality is determined by the skill of the test constructor.	4. Quality is determined largely by skill of the grader reading.
5. Is relatively tedious and difficult to prepare, but easy to score.	5. Is easy to prepare, but relatively tedious and difficult to score.

6. Affords much freedom for test constructor to express his knowledge and values.	6. Affords much freedom for the student to express his knowledge and individuality.
7. States student's tasks and the basis for judgment more clearly.	7. States student's tasks and basis for judgment less clearly.
8. Permits and occasionally encourages guessing.	8. Permits and occasionally encourages bluffing.
9. Distribution of scores is determined by the test.	9. Distribution of scores is controlled largely by the grader-reader.

Similarities

1. Both tests can measure almost any important instructional objective that any written test can measure.

2. Both tests can encourage students to learn concepts, principles, and problem solving.

3. Both tests involve the use of subjective judgment.

4. Both tests yield scores whose value is dependent on objectivity and reliability.

On the basis of these factors, Ebel (1965) proceeds to describe the conditions for the appropriate use of objective and essay tests. Use essay tests under the following five conditions:

1. The group to be tested is small and the test should not be reused.

2. The instructor wishes to do all possible to encourage and reward the development of student skill in written expression.

3. The instructor is more interested in exploring the student's attitudes than in measuring his achievements. (Whether an instructor should be more interested in attitudes than achievement and whether he should expect an honest expression of attitudes in a test he will evaluate seem open to question.)

4. The instructor is more confident of his proficiency as a critical reader than as an imaginative writer of good objective test items.

5. Time available for test preparation is shorter than time available for test grading.

Use objective tests under these conditions:

1. The group to be tested is large or the test may be reused.

2. Highly reliable test scores must be obtained as efficiently as possible.

3. Impartiality of evaluation, absolute fairness, and freedom from halo effects are essential.

4. The instructor is more confident of his ability to express objective test items clearly than of his ability to judge essay test answers correctly.

5. There is more pressure for speedy reporting of scores than for speedy test preparation.

Use either objective or essay tests for the following purposes:

1. Measure almost any important educational achievement which a written test can measure.

2. Test understanding of ability to apply principles.

3. Test ability to think critically.

4. Test ability to solve novel problems.

5. Test ability to select relevant facts and principles, to integrate them toward the solution of complex problems.

6. Encourage students to study for command of knowledge.

Short-Answer Items

The short-answer test item is usually considered the simplest of all item forms. The pupil either responds to a direct question or he inserts words at the appropriate places as directed by the test instructions. Three types of short-answer forms are used by most teachers: (1) the <u>question</u> type; (2) the <u>completion</u> type; and (3) the <u>association</u> type (Blood and Budd, 1972).

<u>The question type</u>. This type consists of a question to which the pupil responds to with a relatively simple answer. An example is:

1. What was the name of the fourth president of the United States?_____

<u>The completion type</u>. This type consists of the familiar fill-in-the blanks exercise. The stem consists of a statement in which one or more words have been left out with a blank in their place. The pupil is directed to fill in the omitted words. An example is:

2. The three colors in the American flag are _____, _____, and _____.

<u>The association type</u>. This type is usually used as part of an exercise involving a number of items that relate to each other by some specified structure or format. The pupil is usually supplied with a word and then asked to supply another word associated with the first in some manner as directed in the instructions on the test. An example is:

Instructions: In the space provided, write the full name of a general associated with a major victory in each period.

1. The Civil War _____

2. World War I_____

3. World War II - Europe_____

4. World War II - Asia_____

The short-answer item is probably most effective in measuring recall or in the testing of specific facts. It has three major weaknesses, however, which must be pointed out: (1) it is extremely difficult to construct items which call for only one correct answer; (2) it stresses rote recall and encourages pupils to spend their time memorizing trivial details rather than seeking broader understandings; and (3) short-answer items are somewhat unrealistic since life problems generally offer a variety of possible solutions rather than one "key-word" solutions (Green, 1963, pp. 27-28).

Since the completion-type item is the type of short-answer items most frequently used by classroom teachers, specific guidelines for writing that type of item will now be discussed. These same guidelines, however, may be used in constructing questions or association-type test items. Payne (1968) suggests the following guidelines for constructing completion-type items.

1. Require short, definite, clear-cut, and explicit answers. An indefinite question statement is likely to lead to scoring problems for instructors and response problems for students.
   Faulty: Ernest Hemingway wrote_____.
   Improved: The Old Man and the Sea was written by
   _____.

2. Avoid multi-mutilated statements. Merely taking a statement, from a text for example, and using blanks liberally can only lead to an ambiguous item. In addition, an instructor is really not sure which portion of the statement an individual is responding to and therefore which objective is being measured. You end up with a nonsensical sequence of blanks.
   Faulty: _____ pointed out in _____ that freedom of thought in America was seriously hampered by _____.
   Improved: That freedom of thought in America was seriously hampered by social pressures toward conformity was pointed out in 1830 by (De Tocqueville).

3. If several correct answers are possible (e.g., synonyms) equal credit should be given to each one.

4. Specify in advance and tell student if scoring will take account of spelling.

5. In testing for comprehension of terms and knowledge of definitions it is often better to provide the term and require a definition rather than provide a definition and require the term. The student is less likely to benefit from verbal association cues if this procedure is followed. In addition, having the student construct the definition is a better measure of his knowledge of it.
   Faulty: What is the general measurement term which describes the consistency with which items in a test are measuring the same thing?
   Improved: Define "internal consistency reliability."

86

6. For completion items it is generally recommended that blanks come at the end of the statement. Beginning an item with a blank is awkward for the student and may interfere with his comprehension of the question. In general, the best approach to item writing is the simple and direct one.

   Faulty: An _____ is the index obtained by dividing a mental age score by chronological age and multiplying by 100.

   Improved: The index obtained by dividing a mental age score by chronological age and multiplying by 100 is called an _____.

7. Minimize the use of textbook expressions or stereotyped language. When statements are taken out of context they tend to become ambiguous. The use of paraphrased statements, however, will reduce the possibility of correct responses that represent meaningless verbal associations. In addition, it should reduce the temptation of pupils to memorize the exact wording of the text or lecture material.

8. Specify the terms in which the response is to be given.

   Faulty: Where does the Security Council of the United Nations hold its meetings?

   Improved: In what city of the United States does the Security Council of the United Nations hold its meetings?

   The requirement that degree of precision is particularly important in mathematics questions stated in free response form. A student may be faced with the problem of trying to out-guess the instructor relative to the degree of error to be tolerated. Is it one decimal place accuracy? Two decimal place accuracy? Different students may come to different conclusions.

   Faulty: If a circle has a 4 inch diameter, the area is _____.

   Improved: A circle has a 4 inch diameter, its area, correct to two decimal places is (12.56) square inches.

9. In general, direct questions are preferable to incomplete declarative sentences.

   Faulty: Gold was discovered in California in the year _____.

   Improved: In what year was gold discovered in California? _____.

10. **Avoid extraneous clues to the correct answer**.
Occasionally the grammatical structure of an item may
lead a student to the correct answer, independent of
his knowledge, particularly if the number of alternative answers is small.

Faulty: A fraction whose denominator is greater
than its numerator is a _____.

Improved: Fractions whose denominators are greater
than their numerators are called _____ fractions.

In the faulty item above, the article "a" functions
as an irrelevant clue. Along this line, blanks
should be of uniform length so that they do not cue
the examinee as to the extensiveness of the expected
response.

Marshall and Hales (1972) suggest the following guidelines
in the form of Do's and Don'ts for writing completion items:

Do

1. Use completion tests to measure lower-order mental
skills.

2. Limit the length of the response to a single word or
short phrase.

3. Use questions which are germane to the area being
measured.

4. Use terms which will have the same meaning to all
examinees.

5. Use terms which all examinees can define and understand.

6. Explicitly state and qualify the question so that a
single response is correct.

7. Make the sentence structure as simple as possible so
that the question will be clear to all examinees.

8. Write the questions in advance so that they can be
analyzed and revised if necessary before the test is
given.

9. Write a comprehensive set of directions.

10. Have all examinees use a prepared answer sheet.

11. Give equal weight to all responses.

12. Construct the answer sheet so that it is easy to score.

13. If possible, use questions rather than incomplete statements.

14. For multiple-response items, have blanks of equal length.

15. Ask only for important information.

16. Inform the examinees in advance that they will be given a completion test. (p. 44)

Don't

1. Overmutilate sentences by leaving too many blanks.

2. Have the answers to a multiple-response item inter-dependent.

3. Ask for non-essentials.

4. Penalize for guessing.

5. Use items which have more than one correct answer.

6. Use questions designed to measure higher-order mental processes.

7. Pull questions verbatim from the textbook or lecture notes. (p. 44)

True-False Items

Although the true-false item type is one of the most widely used of all forms, it is also the most widely misused. The true-false item usually consists of a declarative sentence, to which the pupil responds by marking it true or false. Some examples are:

T F 1. The United States obtained its independence in 1492.

T F 2. World War II ended in 1945.

T F 3. Chemistry is the study of living plants and animals.

T F 4. Fifteen divided by three is six.

The apparent simplicity of the true-false item, however, is deceptive and therefore subject to misuse and abuse. It is in reality one of the most difficult types of items to write properly for two reasons: (1) outside the realms of formal knowledge (i.e., mathematics, grammar, logic) there are few assertions of propositions which can be judged unambiguously true of false; and (2) the deleterious effect that chance or guessing may have upon the response set of the examinee.

Blood and Budd (1972) suggest the following guidelines in the construction and use of true-false items:

1. <u>Do not make your items too long</u>. The major reason for this admonition is that excessive length introduces the irrelevant factor of reading into the item. This is especially true if the added length is due to qualifying words and phrases which the item writer feels are necessary to produce a true statement. In addition to the added burden of reading, with the attendant possibility of ambiguity which this produces, the extra length may provide an irrelevant clue because inexperienced item writers tend to make true statements longer than false statements.

2. <u>Avoid irrelevant clues by specific determiners</u>. A specific determiner is a key word which allows the students to guess the correct answer on the basis of test sophistication when he really does not know the answer. For example, statements which contain the key words "all," "none," "never," "always," "only," or "no" are usually false. Conversely, statements which contain the words "generally," "frequently," "sometimes," "could," "might," or "may" are usually true.

   It is sometimes permissible to take advantage of the tendency of students to use such clues when they do not know the answers if you can use the clue in the reverse way. Take this item, for example:
   T F The sum of the deviations of a set of raw scores from their mean will always equal zero.

   If the student responded to the "always" without knowing the answer, he would miss the item.

3. <u>Avoid irrelevant clues provided by undue specificity in the item</u>. Such statements usually tend to be true. Here is an example:
   T F Twenty-seven nations eventually entered World War I.

4. <u>Avoid negatively worded items</u>. Above all, avoid negatively worded false items. Consider this example:

   T F Knowledge of results does not have a facilitating effect on learning.

   Note that in a straightforward form, i.e., "Knowledge of results has a facilitating effect on learning," it would be a relatively easy item. Worded in a negative fashion, it becomes very puzzling, and even the student who possesses the requisite information might find it difficult to answer.

5. <u>Avoid items containing listings of things some of which may be true and some of which may be false</u>. Take this example from a fourth-grade test:

   T F Sound travels through air, liquids, solids, and vacuums.

6. <u>Test only one point in each item</u>. Particularly, do not have two points, one of which is true and the other false. Here is an example:

   T F Pacific Ocean salmon ascent fresh water rivers to spawn and then descend again to the ocean.

   When such items are keyed "false" there is always the possibility the student may receive credit for erroneous information. Consider this item, for example:

   T F George Washington was first inaugurated President of the U. S. in Philadelphia on April 30, 1789.

   The statement is false since the inauguration was held in New York. Suppose, however, that a student thinks that Philadelphia is correct but that the year was 1791 or that the date was other than April 30. This student, too, will mark the item "false" and will receive credit for the wrong reason.

7. <u>Do not use statements of opinion as the basis for items unless you attribute the opinion to the source</u>.

   T F According to Franklin D. Roosevelt, a balanced budget should be the backbone of the national economy.

   Note that the item in this form really tests whether the student knows the views of the person or the organization in question. If the item were merely a question of opinion without the attribution, it would be improper as a true-false item.

8. <u>Do not "lift" statements from a textbook and expect them to function well as true-false items</u>. In the first place, this practice reinforces the tendency

91

toward rote learning of textual material. In the second place, such statements tend to be true more often than false, and the student may use the stereotyped language as a clue. Take the following example:
T F Feelings ran high in England as a consequence of the Boston Tea Party.

9. <u>Do not use "trick" items where an apparently true statement is rendered false by an insignificant detail</u>. Take the following example:
T F The area of a rectangle 4 ft. by 3 ft. is equal to 12 sq. yds.

10. <u>Avoid any systematic patterning to the answers</u>. Do not use three true items followed by three false items or any other systematic scheme. Incorporate some degree of randomness into the placement of true and false items. Above all, never use all true items or all false items.

11. Use a somewhat larger proportion of false items than true items. The reason for this admonition is that false items tend to be more discriminating than true items. This difference probably occurs because of the mental set with which a student approaches statements containing assertions. If the student does not possess the requisite knowledge to judge the truth or falsity of an assertion, and if the assertion is stated in forceful language, as most true-false items are, the student is more likely to answer true than false because of his conditioned respect for authoritative statements. If the statement is true and the student guesses "true," he will get the item correct when he should not. If the statement is false, however, and he guesses "true," he will miss the item as, in fact, he should.

12. <u>Restrict true-false items to those important assertions which can be reasonably unambiguously judged true or false</u>. The true-false form has been criticized on the basis of the "picky" nature of the knowledge it tests. This occurs because we do not know how to cast our major truths in true-false form. However, the true-false item can be a more versatile approach than it typically now is. We can test not only specific knowledge but also the ability to apply knowledge or principles to novel situations. Consider the following example:

T F   The magnitude of the standard deviation from a
set of scores will be increased by five points if
the magnitude of each of the scores is increased
by five points.

    The true-false form will undoubtedly continue to be
one of the most popular of the item forms. The teacher
should be aware, however, that it is really one of
the most difficult forms to use well. Properly written,
it can be a very effective type of item.

Marshall and Hales (1972) suggest the following <u>Do's</u> and
<u>Don'ts</u> for constructing true-false items:

<u>Do</u>

1. Include enough items to adequately sample the material.

2. Use a Table of Specifications to assure adequate
   sampling.

3. Establish a frame of reference for answering the item.

4. Write concise, unambiguous, and grammatically correct
   statements.

5. Use questions which are germane to the area being tested.

6. Have approximately the same number of true and false
   statements. (p. 75)

<u>Don't</u>

1. Use questions which are partially true or partially
   false.

2. Use unnecessary words or phrases.

3. Have more than one them in the item.

4. Have irrelevant clues.

5. Have a pattern in the order of the responses.

6. Use negative statements.

7. Use the qualifying terms: all, none, some, few, or
   many.

8. Pull statements directly from the textbook or class notes. (p. 76)

Multiple-Choice Items

The multiple-choice item is considered by most test experts to be the best type of objective time for measuring a variety of educational objectives. The item is versatile, and it requires some descriminatory thinking on the part of the pupil. Multiple-choice items have a premise which consists of an incomplete statement or question followed by several distracters. The incomplete statement and question are the most common types. Examples are:

1. The "arithmetic average" is the
   a. Mean
   b. Median
   c. Mode
   d. Average Deviation

2. Who was the author of Tom Sawyer?
   a. John Steinbeck
   b. Ernest Hemingway
   c. Mark Twain
   d. Charles Hailey

Green (1963) suggests the following rules for constructing multiple-choice items:

1. <u>The central problem of the item should be stated in the premise so as to make only one choice justifiable</u>. An item such as the one below permits too great a range of alternative choices to be useful in measurement.
   Faulty Example:
      Ethnic groups are:
         a. artifacts.
         b. cultural groups.
         c. racial groups.
         d. external influences.
         e. language groups.
   Because no problem is presented in the premise of the item above, a variety of choices is possible. A statement such as the following is much superior.
   Example:
      What characteristic best identifies an ethnic group?
         a. Common artifacts.
         b. Shared culture.

94

      c.   Similar racial background.
      d.   Common language.
      e.   Similar appearance

2. **All choices in the item should be grammatically consistent.** Each choice should be grammatically correct as an ending for the premise. As many as possible of the words of the item should be included in the premise to avoid repetition in each choice, as well as to help keep the choices brief.

    Example:
      Why do living organisms need oxygen?
        a.   To purify the blood.
        b.   To oxidize waste.
        c.   To release energy.
        d.   To assimilate food.
        e.   To fight infection.

3. **The choices should be as brief as possible, and the correct response should be neither consistently longer nor shorter than the incorrect responses.**

    Example:
      According to the "natural depravity of man" doctrine of medieval religious groups, man was inherently:
        a.   good.
        b.   evil.
        c.   degraded.
        d.   unreasonable.
        e.   deprived.

4. **A pattern of answers should be avoided.** Teachers tend to make a large number of the correct responses either the first or the last choice. In the process of constructing items, it helps to place the correct choice in the first position, and then when all the items have been constructed, to go back and randomly distribute the correct choices so that each position is used approximately the same number of times.

5. **Negatively stated items should be avoided.**
    Faulty Example:
      Which of the following is not a characteristic of the successful group leader?
        a.   He defines the group purpose.
        b.   He suggests courses of action.
        c.   He shares group experiences.
        d.   He opposes group interests.
        e.   He justifies group actions.

The negative multiple-choice item, just as the negative true-false item, tends to measure reading ability. Poor readers often answer such items incorrectly, even when they know the correct answers.

6. Authority should be quoted when the item contains controversial opinion.
   Example:
   American historians generally agree that the major responsibility for causing World War I lay with:
   a. Germany and Austria.
   b. Germany and Serbia.
   c. Russia and France.
   d. England and France.
   e. Russia and Italy.

If the premise were reworded to read "It is generally agreed that the major responsibility for causing World War I lay with," then there might be several correct answers. For instance, some pupils could argue that German historians generally agree that England and France were responsible. It is unfair to ask the pupil to respond to an opinion item unless he has the reference point of an authority, for he may either disagree with or be unfamiliar with the instructor's opinion.

7. Ambiguous items should be avoided. Each item should contain one clearly stated problem, and unnecessary or unusual words should be avoided. The aim of the teacher should be to write items which all pupils can understand. This rule is perhaps violated more frequently than any other rule for constructing multiple-choice items.
   Faulty Example:
   When there is an active verb in the sentence, the subject does the acting; and when the verb is passive, the subject is acted upon. Which of the following is passive?
   a. Threw.
   b. Hit.
   c. Ran.
   d. Was hit.
   e. Dropped.

Although the item above is not difficult, it is ambiguous because it deals with two problems. It might better be split into two separate items, one dealing with passive verbs and the other with active verbs.

8. <u>All</u> <u>choices</u> <u>should</u> <u>be</u> <u>plausible</u>.
   Faulty Example:
   What is the end punctuation for an interrogative
   sentence?
       a. Exclamation point.
       b. Quotation marks.
       c. Question mark.
       d. Comma.
       e. Semicolon.
   If several of the choices are not plausible, the
   pupil's chances of guessing the correct response are
   increased. In the five-choice item in the example
   above, three of the choices are not plausible; therefore
   the pupil has a 50-50 chance of guessing the correct
   response. In this instance a true-false item would
   have been as useful and much easier to construct.

9. <u>Specific</u> <u>determiners</u> <u>should</u> <u>be</u> <u>avoided</u>.
   Faulty Example:
   The part of speech which tells "how," "when,"
   or "where" is an:
       a. noun.
       b. pronoun.
       c. adverb.
       d. conjunction.
       e. verb.
   Obviously <u>adverb</u> is the correct answer because it is
   the only choice which begins with a vowel. A grammatical clue such as <u>a</u> or <u>an</u> preceding a choice aids the
   pupil who does not know the correct response.

10. <u>Each</u> <u>item</u> <u>should</u> <u>contain</u> <u>an</u> <u>independent</u> <u>problem</u> <u>which</u>
    <u>gives</u> <u>no</u> <u>clues</u> <u>to</u> <u>the</u> <u>answers</u> <u>of</u> <u>other</u> <u>items</u>. Fre-
    quently teachers include in a test items which are
    interrelated and therefore give clues to the answers
    of several items in the group.
    Faulty Example:
    When did the American Civil War begin?
        a. 1812.
        b. 1860.
        c. 1861.
        d. 1875.
        e. 1885.
    The Morrill Act passed by Congress during the
    Civil War authorized land grants for the es-
    tablishment of:
        a. state universities.
        b. agricultural and mechanical colleges.

c. junior colleges.
d. medical colleges.
e. normal schools.

Although the pupil may not know the date of the Civil War, he may know the date of the Morrill Act, which the second item relates to the Civil War; thus he may answer the first item correctly simply because of the clue in the second item.

Marshall and Hales(1972) suggest the following guidelines for multiple-choice items:

Do

1. Use multiple-choice tests to measure higher-order mental processes.

2. Include enough items to adequately sample the material.

3. Use a Table of Specifications to ensure adequate sampling.

4. Establish a frame of reference for answering the item in the stem.

5. Express the problem in the stem.

6. Write concise, unambiguous, and grammatically correct items.

7. Use questions which are germane to the area being measured.

8. Incorporate in the stem all words which would otherwise need to appear in each alternate.

9. Adhere to any logical ordering of the alternates which might exist.

10. Provide about the same number of keyed responses in each choice position on the total test.

11. Control the difficulty of the item by the homogeneity of the responses.

12. Make every foil appealing to the students who do not know the correct answer. (p. 67)

<u>Don't</u>

1. Use multiple-choice tests to measure writing skill or creativity.

2. Have conflicting frames of reference embedded in the same item.

3. Have grammatical errors in the item.

4. Be ambiguous.

5. Provide superfluous information in the item.

6. Have clang associations between keyed response and the stem.

7. Have long keyed responses and short foils or the reverse.

8. Have a pattern in the rotation of the keyed responses among the choice positions.

9. Use unnecessary, technical terminology.

10. Include poor foils in an item.

11. Use "none of the above" or "all of the above" as alternatives in "best" answer items. (p. 67)

Matching Items

The matching test, a favorite for many years of elementary school teachers, also has applications at the upper levels. The matching test consists of a column of items on the left-hand side of the page and a column of options on the right. The pupil's job is to select the option that is correctly associated with the item. Much learning involves this association act: names and dates, foreign words and their English translation, parts of a machine and their function, etc. The matching test is most applicable to this type of learning. It does, however, have some limitations: (1) it is not readily adaptable to the higher levels in the taxonomy of educational objectives; and (2) although easy to construct, pupils find it relatively time-consuming to take.

Chase (1974) suggests the following guidelines for making the matching test a sharper instrument:

1. The format that seems to facilitate taking the test calls for the stimulus items to be listed and numbered in a column on the left of the page, whereas the options to be associated with the items are listed and lettered in a column at the right. Naturally, the list of options should contain more possible responses than required to complete the test. In this way the last item is not answered by the student's simply having used all options except one.

2. Each matching exercise should contain only homogeneous material. In this way we increase the likelihood that all options appear plausible for all items. An example of the problem of not having homogeneous material might look like this:

1. Boston	a) the first capital city of the United States
2. Charles Pinckney	b) the place where tea was dumped into the ocean as a protest against taxation
:	
:	:
	:
5. Philadelphia	h) a signer of the US constitution
	i) one of the 13 original colonies

If Pinckney's name appears among a list of cities and other geographical sites, we can select (h) as the correct answer simply by elimination. It is the only item that could be matched logically with a person. If this exercise had contained only cities and towns, this test-taking skill would not have yielded that one point on the score in absence of the necessary historical knowledge.

3. Ease of taking the matching test is facilitated if the items and options are arranged in a systematic order. Dates should be in chronological order, whereas names of people, nomenclature of mechanisms, etc. should be in alphabetical order. This reduces the amount of searching necessary for the student to locate responses. It also negates the occasional student hypothesis that the test has been arranged so as to provide a pattern in the answers.

4. All items and options for a given matching exercise should be on a single page. This eliminates the possibility of students' overlooking options that may be on a second page. It also reduces the likelihood

of random errors being made by students as a result of turning pages back and forth.

5. <u>The number of items in a single matching exercise should be limited to five or six in the lower grades and to 10 to 15 as a maximum at upper levels.</u> If more matches are desired, arrange for several matching exercises within a single examination. Ideally, each exercise should be limited to the prescribed number of items and should explore a different topic from other exercises, thereby providing a wider sampling of knowledge of the topic being studied.

6. <u>Students should know exactly how the matching is to be done.</u> Instructions should tell the student whether he can use an option more than once, whether each item has only one correct answer, and how the marking is to be done. With primary school children, marking is best done by drawing lines from the item to its correct answer although this procedure is difficult to score. With older children, a line can be drawn to the left of each item, with the letter of the selected option to be written on the line. This makes scoring by key quite easy. Here is a two-item portion of a matching test illustrating this procedure.

  <u>b</u> 1. Henry Clay   a) senator from South Carolina
  <u> </u> 2. Daniel Webster b) senator from Kentucky

Marshall and Hales (1971) suggest the following guidelines which relate to matching items:

<u>Do</u>

1. Use a Table of Specifications to insure adequate sampling.

2. Establish a frame of reference for answering the item in the premise.

3. Establish a general orientation in the introductory statement.

4. Be clear and concise.

5. Use correct grammar.

6. Adhere to a logical ordering of alternates if one exist.

7. Control the difficulty of the item by the homogeneity of the alternates.

8. Have homogeneous premises and homogeneous alternates.

9. Inform the examinees if an alternate may be used more than once.

10. Use for who, what, when, or where situations. (pp. 133-134)

Don't

1. Expect to measure higher-order mental processes.

2. Have errors of grammar in premises or alternates.

3. Provide superfluous information.

4. Have clang associations between keyed responses and premises.

5. Have a pattern between the order of appearance of premises and keyed responses.

6. Use unnecessary, technical terminology.

7. Have more than twelve alternatives.

8. Have an equal number of premises and alternatives. (p. 134)

Essay Items

The essay test item usually consists of questions beginning with or including such directions as "discuss," "explain," "outline," "evaluate," "define," and "describe." Although not used as frequently as objective-type items, it is still, nevertheless widely used. The advantages of the essay item may be listed as follows: (1) it is applicable to measurement of writing, organizational ability and creativeness; (2) it is relatively easy to construct; and (3) it promotes proper study habits. The major disadvantages are: (1) it gives a limited test sample; (2) it is difficult to grade and evaluate; (3) it is subject to low reliability both between examinations and between evaluators; (4) it favors the verbally articulate pupil; and (5) it encourages bluffing (Green, 1963, p. 5).

Noll and Scannell (1972) make the following suggestions for improving and scoring essay items:

1. Define and restrict the field or area to be covered by the question.

2. The teacher should give more time and thought to the preparation of essay questions.

3. Students should be told in advance what type of examination they will be given.

4. The value or weight of each question should be indicated.

5. The quality of handwriting, spelling, grammar, punctuation, and clarity of thought should be checked and should carry weight in the evaluation of every essay or composition assigned by English or foreign-language teachers.

6. Errors in spelling, grammar, usage, etc. should be checked in students' written work by every teacher but should not affect the mark or grade except in language classes.

7. Prepare enough questions to sample the learning of the students adequately.

8. Optional questions giving pupils a choice should not be provided. Such questions reduce the comparability of the sampling of pupils' learning and therefore of the basis for scoring. (pp. 202-208)

In terms of improving the grading of essay questions, Noll and Scannell list the following suggestions:

1. Determine in advance the methods to be used to score the answers.

2. Write answers to each question before administering the test.

3. Remove or cover all pupil-identifying data on papers to be read.

4. Read all papers for one question at a time instead of reading each paper in its entirety.

5. If a number of different factors, for example, accuracy, methods used, possibly correctness and ease

of expression, are to be taken into account, evaluate each separately.

6. After a set of papers has been graded lay them aside for several hours a day and then look them over again.

Marshall and Hales (1972) list the following Do's and Don'ts for essay items:

Do

1. Use essay tests to measure higher-order mental processes.

2. Include enough questions to adequately sample the material.

3. Limit the length of the response.

4. Use questions which are germane to the area being measured.

5. Use terms which will have the same meaning to all examinees.

6. Use terms which all examinees can define and understand.

7. Use questions which pose problems to be solved.

8. Explicitly state and qualify the problem so that it will be interpreted in the same manner by all examinees.

9. Make the sentence structure as simple as possible so the problem posed will be clear to all examinees.

10. Write the question in advance so that it can be analyzed and revised if necessary before the test is given.

11. Write a comprehensive set of directions and include in these directions the weight of each question.

12. Write a model set of answers.

13. Before scoring the papers, determine the weights of the various elements expected in a complete answer.

14. Require the examinees to answer every question on the test.

15. Read a response and make a gross judgment as to its relative worth.

16. Score one question for all papers before going to the next question.

17. Score a question only on the achievement being measured.

18. Add the scores for each question to determine a paper's total worth.

19. Ignore the names of the examinees when grading.

20. Inform the examinees in advance that they will be given an essay test.

21. Analyze past questions. (pp. 34-35)

Don't

1. Judge papers on extraneous factors such as handwriting, spelling, and grammar.

2. Make a general estimate of a paper's total worth as a first step in scoring.

3. Construct a test containing too few items to adequately sample the material.

4. Use optional questions.

5. Use different questions if the examinees are to be compared.

6. Use questions designed to elicit only factual information.

7. Expect the students to know the intent of the question unless it is explicitly stated.

8. Allow students to write "verbal garbage" with the hope of stumbling on the right answer. (p. 35)

THE ORAL EXAMINATION

There are four types of oral examinations: (1) orally administered examinations which require an oral response and include those in which single questions are asked individuals in a group situation and those in which numerous questions are posed to a single individual; (2) orally administered examinations which require a written response; (3) orally administered examination of the standardized type including intelligence tests and personality measures; and (4) interviews in which persons are selected for particular responsibilities or positions.

Green (1963) suggests the following principles which should be used in using the oral examination:

1. The teacher should read the questions loudly and slowly and enunciate carefully.

2. The type of oral examination should be adaptable to the field in which it is used.

3. When the oral examination is used primarily for teaching or review purposes, little or no grading weight should be given to the examination.

4. When only one question is asked each pupil, care must be taken to keep all questions comparable in difficulty or at least to adjust the difficulty of the question to the competence of the pupil.

5. Although grading of oral exams is usually subjective, an effort should be made to eliminate the influence of extraneous factors such as favoritism. (pp. 79-81)

Green (1963, p. 5) also lists the strengths and weaknesses of the oral examination:

Strengths	Weaknesses
1. Gives extensive measurement.	1. Is too time-consuming.
2. Is useful as an instructional device.	2. Results in poor pupil performance due to lack of practice.
3. Permits teacher to give cues to elicit desired responses.	3. Provides limited sample unless pupils are tested frequently.

4. Improves test rapport for pupils who fear written examinations.	4. Is frequently poorly planned. 5. Is not subject to refinement. 6. Gives poor comparative evaluation of pupils.

Marshall and Hales (1971) suggest the following Do's and Don'ts for oral examinations:

Do

1. Include enough questions to adequately sample the material.

2. Limit the length of the response.

3. Limit the length of the question.

4. Use questions which are germane to the area of skill being measured.

5. If applicable, use unfamiliar material in performance tests.

6. Use terms that all examinees can define and understand.

7. Use terms that will have the same meaning to all examinees.

8. Explicitly state and qualify the question so that it will be interpreted in the same manner by all examinees.

9. Make the sentence structure as simple as possible so that the questions will be clear to all examinees.

10. Prepare the questions in advance so that they can be analyzed and revised if necessary before the test is given.

11. Write a comprehensive set of directions.

12. Write a model set of answers.

13. Read the directions and questions to the examinees using a clear, distinct voice.

14. Use an oral-response test primarily with individuals.

15. Use a rating-scale or check-list for scoring an oral-response test.

16. Use the sorting method or point-score method for scoring a written-response test.

17. Inform the examinees in advance that they will be given an oral test.

18. Use the same questions if the examinees' performances are to be compared. (pp. 90-91)

Don't

1. Judge responses on extraneous factors.

2. Evaluate a student by his responses to just a few questions.

3. Use different questions if the examinees are to be compared.

4. Allow students to respond with "verbal garbage" hoping to stumble on the right answer.

5. Ask for nonessentials.

6. Use an oral-response test for measuring individual achievement in a large group.

7. Assign grades to the responses if using an oral-response test as a review. (p. 91)

Chapter VI

APPRAISING TEACHER-MADE TESTS:
ANALYZING TEST ITEMS

Once a teacher-made test has been constructed,
administered, scored, and pupils have been assigned grades
(at least on a tentative basis), the teacher may feel that
his job is complete. However, whether his job is finished or
not depends on the extent to which the test could be considered
to be a good test. The teacher attempted to follow good test
construction procedures including formulating objectives,
constructing a test blueprint, adhering to accepted principles
for item-writing, etc. But the questions still remain: Was
it a valid and effective test for its intended purpose? Was
the test reliable and consistent in what it was intended to
measure?

The answers to these questions can be arrived more precisely through statistical procedures referred to as <u>item</u>
<u>analysis</u> and the <u>coefficient</u> <u>of</u> <u>reliability</u>. The focus in
this chapter is on <u>item</u> <u>analysis</u> which can give the teacher
a more objective indication of the validity of his test.
This procedure also enables the teacher to ascertain how he
might improve his test as well as what items may need revising
or discarding. Establishing the reliability of the teacher-
made test will also be discussed, but to a lesser extent than
item analysis.

ITEM ANALYSIS

<u>Item</u> <u>analysis</u> is defined as the re-examintion of indivi-
dual test items to determine their strengths and weaknesses.
Item analysis typically focuses on two major questions with
respect to each item: (1) How difficult was each test item
for the entire class? and (2) To what extent did each item
differentiate between those pupils who did well as opposed
to those pupils who did poorly on the test? The answer to
the first question is obtained through the computation of a
<u>level</u> <u>of</u> <u>difficulty</u> (also called <u>index</u> <u>of</u> <u>difficulty</u>); the
answer to the latter question is obtained by computing an
<u>index</u> <u>of</u> <u>discrimination</u>. Prior to discussing the computation
of the level of difficulty and the index of discrimination,
however, it is necessary to present the preliminary procedure
for setting up an item analysis.

Setting Up For An Item Analysis

Once the teacher has administered and scored a test, he should follow this procedure:

1. Arrange the tests in numerical order (ordinal ranking) with the highest scoring papers on top and the lowest on the bottom.

2. Divide the ordinally ranked papers into two groups or piles to determine the two extreme groups in the distribution of scores. Most theorists in test construction tend to obtain the two extreme groups on the basis of the upper 27% of the scores and the lower 27% of the scores. Storey (1970; p. 84) summarizes four different methods for dividing the two extreme groups (this is called dichotomizing) which are adapted below:

Method	Lower Group	Upper Group	Order of Merit	Practicality
a. 50-50	lowest 50%	Upper 50%	2	1
b. 16-16	lowest 16%	Upper 16%	4	3
c. 13.5-13.5	those between -1σ and -2σ	those between $+1\sigma$ and $+2\sigma$	1	4
d. 27-27	lowest 27%	Upper 27%	3	2

This author prefers the 27-27 split over the 50-50 split because of the saving work necessary to obtain the response data for the middle 46 per cent of the scores that are omitted when using this method.

Now that the preliminary steps have resulted in two groups of papers, the high-scoring 27 per cent and the low-scoring 27%, the teacher should now proceed to compute the difficulty index and the discrimination index for each item.

Difficulty Index

The difficulty index of an item is the percentage of pupils who score or answer each item correctly. It is found by converting the total number of students responding correctly to a proportion of the entire class.

$$P = \frac{N_c}{N_t} \times 100$$

Where:

P = level of difficulty expressed as a percentage

N_c = number of students who answer an item correctly

N_t = total number of students who attempt an item

To obtain N_c in the numerator above, it is also necessary to include the number of pupils in the middle 46% group (which are not being used in the item analysis per se) who answered each item correctly.

To illustrate, let us suppose that an item is answered correctly by twenty-four of thirty-five pupils who attempt to answer it. The difficulty index is:

$$P = \frac{24}{35} \times 100$$

$$= 68$$

This means that 68 per cent of the pupils who attempted the item answered it correctly.

Test theorists suggest that a test designed to obtain maximum differentiation among pupils should be of 50 per cent difficulty; thus a test containing 100 items should have a mean of 50. Generally speaking, then, items should cluster in the vicinity of 50%. In actual practice, a range of difficulty of 25-80% is allowed. According to Storey (1970; p. 87) items at or below the .25 level of difficulty are discarded because they are (1) too difficult for the group; (2) likely to be unduly influenced by guessing; (3) will likely fail to discriminate since good students are generally no more skilled at guessing than poor ones; and (4) even if the very difficult items should discriminate satisfactorily, they do so on the basis of too few examinees. Items with difficulty indexes at or above .80 should be discarded because they are too easy for the group and are also unlikely to discriminate adequately.

Discrimination Index

The discrimination index of a test item indicates its ability to differentiate between students of high achievement and students of low achievement.

Test items can be classified as either:

1. Positively discriminating - an item in which the percentage of correct answers is higher in the upper group than in the lower group.

2. Negatively discriminating - an item in which the percentage of correct answers is higher for the lower group than for the upper group.

3. Nondiscriminating - an item in which the percentage of correct answers is the same for both groups.

The computation of the discrimination is derived from the formula:

$$D = \frac{U-L}{N}$$

Where:

D = index of discrimination
U = number of students in upper group who successfully answer the item
L = number of students in lower group who successfully answer the item
N = number of students in upper or lower group

To illustrate, let us assume that nine of fourteen pupils in the upper group (upper 27%) answered an item correctly, while three of fourteen in the lower group (lower 27%) answer the item incorrectly. The discrimination index is:

$$D = \frac{9-3}{14} = +.43$$

The maximum size of the discrimination index is +1.00, while the minimum size is -1.00. Maximum discrimination occurs when the index is plus; minimum discrimination occurs when a negative index occurs. Any negative value means that the test item discriminates, to some degree, in the wrong direction. Therefore, the discriminating power is unsatisfactory. Positive values show that the test item discriminates in the desired direction, even though it may not be completely satisfactory (Ahman and Glock, 1967; p. 189).

The following guidelines are offered for the interpretation and use of the discrimination index:

Value of D	Description	Suggestions
+.40 or higher	High positive discrimination	Keep item
+.20 - +.39	Moderate positive discrimination	Revise apparent weaknesses in item; try item again
+.10 - +.19	Low positive discrimination	Item should be discarded

Further suggestions:

1. A good achievement test should have about 50% of the items exceeding +.40.

2. Less than 40% should have values between +.40 and +.20.

3. Less than 10% between +.20 and .00.

4. None should have negative values.

Table VIII adapted from Storey (1970) gives some examples of items which have been analyzed and decisions made with respect to retaining, discarding or revising some test items.

Reliability

The teacher has in the process of running the item analysis now established more objectively whether the test is a good one and if it discriminates between the high-scoring and the low-scoring pupils. He should now also determine the reliability of his test or establish the extent to which the test measures consistently what it purports to measure. One of the simplest and quickest ways for him to establish the reliability of a test is through Kuder and Richardson's (1937) formula:

TABLE VIII

ITEM ANALYSIS SHEET

Item No.	Group	Response				% Cor.	% Cor.	Item difficulty	Item discrimination	Action	Reasons for Action
		A	B	C	D						
1	U	4	5	41*	0	82	62	.62**	.61***	retain	All the distractors working, discriminates well between the two extreme groups.
	L	13	10	21	6	42					
12	U	16	10	4	20*	40	39	.39	.02	discard	Although distractors working and difficulty level acceptable, it does not discriminate. It is suspected of being invalid. Should not be counted in scoring test.
	L	13	11	7	19	38					
13	U	45*	3	0	2	90	81	.81	.43	revise	Tends to be easy but all distractors working and it discriminates well. Alternative (c) should be more plausible. Count in scoring exam anyway.
	L	36	6	2	5	72					
17	U	26*	14	0	10	52	30	.30	.73	retain	A difficult but good item.
	L	4	13	13	20	08					
19	U	0	49*	1	0	98	94	.94	.08	discard	Too easy and low, if not poor, discrimination index.
	L	0	45	3	2	90					

TABLE VIII (Cont'd.)

Item No.	Group	Response A	B	C	D	% Cor.	% Cor.	Item difficulty	Item discrimination	Action	Reasons for Action
24	U	20*	10	11	9	40	42	.42	-.07	discard	Discriminates against upper group. Is discarded and scores earned on it not used in present test.
	L	22	9	10	9	44					
28	U	0	0	20	30*	60	52	.52	.24	discard	One distractor not working; low discrimination index.
	L	0	2	26	22	44					
39	U	2	3	45*	0	90	80	.80	.45	revise	Distractor (d) not working; revision would make distractor (d) more plausible. This should also increase the item's difficulty.
	L	7	8	35	0	70					

* = correct response; ** = $\dfrac{\text{total percent correct}}{2}$; *** = read from special table and may not yield same results as D formula.

From THE MEASUREMENT OF CLASSROOM LEARNING by Arthur G. Storey
© 1970, Science Research Associates, Inc. Reprinted by permission of the publisher.

$$r_t = \frac{n(s^2t) - M(n-M)}{s_t^2 (n - 1)}$$

Where:

r_t = reliability of the test

n = number of items in the test

s_t = standard deviation of the group on the scores on the test

M = mean of the scores on the test

To illustrate, let us again make reference to the statistics derived for the 100-item Biology Test which were computed in Chapter III. This test showed the following data:

n = 100 items

s_t = 11

M = 73

$$r_t = \frac{100(11^2)-73(100-73)}{11^2(100-1)}$$

$$= \frac{(100)(121)-73(27)}{121(99)}$$

$$= \frac{12100-1971}{11979}$$

$$= \frac{10129}{11979}$$

$$= .85$$

A perusal of Table IV in Chapter III suggests that a reliability coefficient of .85 denotes a strong and direct degree of association and so we can infer that we have a highly reliable test which measures consistently what it is supposed to measure.

The Standard Error of Measurement

While a reliability coefficient indicates the degree to which a test is consistent, it is also important for the teacher to know the reliability of the individual test scores for each pupil. The reliability of a given test score is called the standard error of measurement (SE_meas). This index gives us an estimate of the accuracy of a single raw score on a test whose reliability coefficient and standard deviation are known. More specifically, the SE_{meas} gives the teacher the extent to which or the probability that a pupil's actual or obtained raw score does not differ too much from his <u>true</u> <u>score</u>. The formula for the standard error of measurement is:

$$SE_{meas} = \sigma \sqrt{1-r_t}$$

Where:

σ = the standard deviation of the test

r_t = the reliability of the test

To illustrate, the standard deviation for the 100-item Biology Test used in Chapter III was 11, while the reliability of the test was .85. Using the formula, we have

$$SE_{meas} = 11\sqrt{1-.85}$$
$$= 11\sqrt{.15}$$
$$= 11(.39)$$
$$= 4.29$$
$$= 4$$

The answer ($SE_{meas} = 4$) suggests that 68 chances out of 100 (68/100 or 2/3) any obtained raw score will not vary from its specific true score by more than 4 points. More specifically, the chances are about two to one that the true score of an individual who makes a raw score of 86 on the Biology Test, for example, will be between 82 and 90. One SE_{meas} is analogous to one standard deviation. The SE_{meas} is in fact an estimate of the standard deviation of a group of scores were the individual to be tested repeatedly on the same test. This of course is impractical and therefore not done.

The SE_{meas} should always be used in interpreting an individual's obtained score.

Chapter VII

COMMERCIALLY-MADE TESTS: STANDARDIZED TESTS

Teacher-made tests discussed in the two preceding chapters are but one major type of testing device used by the classroom teacher. This type of measurement device typically uses a comparative group composed of pupils in the same classroom or grade. The comparison of pupils with other representative groups of pupils on a national, regional, state, or local base is made by using standardized tests. Standardized tests, in contrast to teacher-made tests, are typically produced by commercial test companies. Classroom teachers should understand commercially-made or standardized tests in order to use them as another major type of measurement device in evaluating pupil growth.

DEFINITION

Adams (1964) suggests that the term "standardized test" has come to signify a measuring instrument with the following characteristics:

1. Specific directions for administering the test are stated in detail, usually including even the exact words to be used by the examiner in giving instructions and specifying exact time limits. By following the directions, teachers and counselors in many schools can administer the test in essentially the same way.

2. Specific directions are provided for scoring. Usually a scoring key is supplied that reduces scoring to merely comparing the answers with the key; little or nothing is left to the judgment of the scorer. Sometimes carefully selected samples are provided with which a student's product is to be compared.

3. Norms are supplied to aid in interpreting the scores.

4. Information needed for judging the value of the test is provided. Before the test becomes available for purchase, research is conducted to study its reliability and validity.

5. A manual is supplied that explains the purposes and uses of the test.

Thorndike (1969) describes a standardized test in the following terms:

> The word "standardized" in a test title means only that all students answer the same questions and a large number of questions under uniform directions and uniform time limits, and that there is a uniform or standard reference group to the performance of which a student's performance can be compared. The term "standardized" does not mean that the test measures what should or could be taught at a particular grade level, or that the test provides "standards of achievement" that students should or could reach at a particular grade level. All that a standardized test does is describe present performance on a uniform set of tasks administered, presumably, under uniform conditions, either for an individual student or the students in a school system. The description is basically in relative terms, that is, in relation to the performance of a sample carefully chosen to represent some more delimited norm group. But a somewhat more absolute interpretation can be arrived at by examining the specific tasks that pupils are and are not able to handle. (p. 257)

The same source (Thorndike and Hagen, 1969) then proceeds to differentiate between standardized and teacher-made tests as shown in Table IX.

The steps in the construction of a standardized test are similar to those used in constructing a teacher-made test. Tinkelman (1971) lists the procedures involved in constructing a standardized test:

1. Developing test specifications.

2. Writing the test items.

3. Pretesting the items and analyzing the item statistics.

4. Compiling the preliminary test forms.

5. Trying out the preliminary test forms to verify time limits, difficulty, reliability, etc.

6. Compiling the final test forms.

TABLE IX

DIFFERENCES BETWEEN STANDARDIZED AND TEACHER-MADE TESTS

Standardized Achievement Test	Teacher-made Test
1. Based on content and objectives common to many schools throughout the country.	1. Based on content and objectives specific to teacher's own class or school.
2. Deals with large segments of knowledge or skill, usually with only a few items appraising any one skill or topic.	2. May deal either with a specific limited topic or skill or with larger segments of knowledge and skill.
3. Developed with the help of professional writers, reviewers, and editors of test items.	3. Developed usually by one teacher with little or no outside help.
4. Uses items that have been tried out, analyzed, and revised before becoming part of the test.	4. Uses items that have rarely been tried out, analyzed, or revised before becoming part of the test.
5. Has high reliability typically.	5. Has moderate or low reliability typically.
6. Provides norms for various groups that are broadly representative of performance throughout the country.	6. Limited usually to the class or a single school as a reference group.

From R. L. Thorndike and E. Hagen, Measurement and Evaluation in Psychology and Education (New York: John Wiley and Sons, Inc., 1969). Used with permission.

7. Administering the final test forms for standardi-
    zation purposes.

8. Preparing norms, a test manual, and supplementary
    test materials.

9. Printing and publication.

TYPES OF STANDARDIZED TESTS

Most standardized tests used in Education are generally
grouped in five general classifications: achievement,
intelligence (mental ability), special aptitude, personality,
and interest. Relating the objectives of the testing program to what the tests are capable of measuring is most
important. The following brief descriptions of tests will
help to determine what type of test to use for a specific
purpose. Examples of each of the five categories of
standardized tests are provided at the end of this chapter.

Achievement Tests

1. Serve as a yardstick for pupil and teacher in
    measuring progress toward proposed goals.

2. Point out to the pupil and teacher the degree of
    efficiency of tasks performed in the various
    subject matter areas as a result of specific
    instruction.

3. Indicate, in a diagnostic way, assets and liabilities
    in the pupil's academic life as they relate to the
    various subject matter areas.

Intelligence (Mental Ability) Tests

1. Indicate the level of academic attainment one may
    expect from pupils.

2. Point out discrepancies in the pupil's measured
    abilities and subject matter achievement.

3. Aid in determining additional academic accomplish-
    ments that may be within the reach of the pupil.

Special Aptitude Tests

1. Help in determining the pupil's chances of success
    in academic and nonacademic courses and future
    occupations.

121

2. Indicate special talents which may be worthy of
    development.

3. Provide the pupil with objective evidence which helps
    him to think critically of himself in relation to his
    future.

4. Point out assets and liabilities in the pupil which
    may be strengthened or compensated.

Personality Inventories

1. Help in pin-pointing certain areas of maladjustment.

2. Assist the student toward better self understanding.

3. Are self-report devices.

4. Measures non-intellective aspects of the individual.

Interest Inventories

1. Point out occupational areas which involve activities
    for which the pupil has expressed a preference.

2. Indicate discrepancies in expressed and measured
    interests.

3. May reveal fields of activity which might otherwise
    be overlooked.

4. Are self-report devices.

The _Seventh Mental Measurements Yearbook_ by Buros (1972)
provides another scheme for classifying standardized tests as
shown in Table X.

USES OF STANDARDIZED TESTS

The following are some of the values of standardized
testing that should be understood by the entire professional
staff of a school.

1. Tests can aid in identifying learning problems of boys
    and girls. Tests having a number of subtests which
    measure a variety of traits or skills enable the
    teacher or counselor to further identify learning
    difficulties. To pinpoint the difficulty a student
    is having, an analysis of the test questions missed
    is necessary.

TABLE X

CLASSIFICATION OF TESTS IN THE SEVENTH
MENTAL MEASUREMENTS YEARBOOK (1972)

VOLUME I

VOLUME II

From O. K. Buros, editor, The Seventh Mental Measurements Yearbook
(Highland Park, New Jersey: Gryphon Press, 1972). Used with
permission.

2. Tests can help in determining expectancy levels of boys and girls. Expectancy level as used here refers to the capability of the pupil.

3. Tests can assist in evaluating the pupil's skill mastery in many subject areas.

4. Interest inventories can give additional clues of pupil's interests. They may verify stated interests or indicate discrepancies between stated and measured interest.

5. Personality inventories can help in estimating pupil adjustment in many areas of life. Personality inventories may be administered, particularly on an individual basis, to determine the degree of maladjustment. It is also possible to use the items from the inventory in an interview situation to help pupils with their difficulties.

6. Tests can help in making comparisons of what the pupil is capable of doing with what he is doing in school. By comparing measured ability with achievement scores, it is possible to determine whether the pupil is experiencing achievement difficulties. The scattergram may be used for graphic indication of discrepancies between measured ability and achievement. Although this technique identifies the pupils who fall outside the normal expectation level, other techniques must be used to find out "why" they are having difficulties.

7. Tests can be used in the grouping of pupils for instructional purposes. Intelligence and achievement tests may be used for this purpose to supplement the academic records and teacher judgments and recommendations.

8. Tests can be of assistance in selecting appropriate instructional materials for pupils. For pupils to profit most from instructional materials, these materials must be on their ability, achievement, and interest levels.

9. Tests can aid in evaluating various aspects of a school's instructional program. A comprehensive look at the achievement test results for the various subject areas at a particular grade level and the relationship to area and national norms will point

out strong and weak areas in the program of instruction. In determining the anticipated progress for a class, intelligence tests need to be employed.

10. Tests can help in identifying pupils in need of special attention. Additional investigation may indicate that the condition could be improved through some kind of special program.

11. Tests can help in gaining a better understanding of themselves. Wiser choices and decisions on the part of pupils are possible when pupils have a better understanding of themselves.

12. Tests can assist in planning a pupil's educational and vocational program. When the pupil reaches the point where he is permitted to select a training program leading toward a future educational or vocational goal, extensive planning is a vital necessity. Ability, achievement, interest, and special aptitude tests can be of great assistance in this regard.

Hedges (1969) lists ten major reasons why tests have value and should be used in the elementary school which may apply to their usefulness in the secondary school as well:

1. Pre-testing helps the teacher know where and how to begin.

2. Pre-testing frequently identifies those students in need of remedial help.

3. Pre-testing provides a basis for flexible grouping in particular skill areas.

4. Pre-testing coupled with post-testing tells the teacher how much the students have improved.

5. Test information helps the teacher to know the extent to which he is succeeding.

6. Test information provides a basis for student self-assessment and motivation.

7. Testing is one of the techniques of teaching.

8. Test scores provide a basis for normative comparison

with other students and with community, state, or even national norms.

9. Test information provides one means of communicating intelligently with parents about a child's progress in terms of the child's capacity.

10. Testing helps provide a basis for communicating with parents.

11. Test data furnish a basis for detecting, and hence for attempting to remedy, certain weaknesses in the curriculum. (p. 1)

Of vital importance to the classroom teacher are the uses of achievement test results as suggested by Horrocks and Schoonover (1968):

1. To gain a picture of the range and nature of individual differences in a group where some specified aspect of achievement is concerned.

2. To equate groups for research and sectioning purposes.

3. To determine an examinee's level of achievement in relation to his age and ability.

4. To provide a basis for selection, promotion, and termination.

5. To group students into relatively homogeneous groups for instructional purpose.

6. To determine rate of progress by comparing present and past achievement.

7. To diagnose learning difficulties.

8. To evaluate the results of a method of instruction.

9. To evaluate teachers' success in teaching students.

10. To provide a basis for counseling with parents as well as with students.

11. To provide a basis for grading.

12. To compare the status of instructional units (schools,

126

classrooms, cities, counties, states, etc.).

13. To diagnose a given school's strengths and weaknesses.

14. To evaluate new school entrants

15. To determine, in part, the efficacy of certain administrative policies.

16. To predict future success as well as present readiness.

17. To act as an adjunct to instruction and as a teaching tool.

18. To act as a motivation device. (pp. 95-96)

As a rule, classroom teachers will find a larger place for nonstandardized, teacher-made tests in dealing with instructional problems than will school administrators in dealing with administrative problems. The reverse condition will tend to be true for standardized tests. Table XI is a sort of "balance sheet" provided by Stanley (1964) which briefly summarizes some of the chief advantages and limitations of various types of achievement tests. This summary brings into perspective the value of both standardized and teacher-made tests.

MINIMAL TESTING PROGRAMS

It is somewhat difficult to determine the types and number of standardized tests that should be administered to pupils within a specific school system. Since the major purpose of tests is to help the teacher in evaluating pupil progress, however, it is possible to deal generally with the relative importance of the various categories of standardized tests. Two prototypic minimal testing programs have been suggested by Green (1970) and Lien (1971) and are shown in Tables XII and XIII.

SELECTING STANDARDIZED TESTS

Assuming that a school defines its testing needs, knows what kinds of tests are to be given, and at what grade levels at what times of the year, the question arises as to which test to select from among the many available. The following brief suggestions are offered by Shertzer and Stone (1966) for those attempting to select standardized tests:

TABLE XI

Advantages and Limitations of Standardized And Nonstandardized Tests of Achievement

	STANDARDIZED		NONSTANDARDIZED			
			Essay		Objective	
Criterion	Advantages	Limitations	Advantages	Limitations	Advantages	Limitations
1. Validity						
a. Curricular	Careful selection by competent persons. Fit typical situations.	Inflexible. Too general in scope to meet local requirements fully, especially in unusual situations.	Useful for English, advanced classes; afford language training. May encourage sound study habits.	Limited sampling. Bluffing is possible. Mix language factor in all scores.	Extensive sampling of subject matter. Flexible in use. Discourages bluffing.	Narrow sampling of functions tested. Negative learning possible.
b. Statistical	With best tests, high.	Criteria often inappropriate or unreliable. Size of coefficients dependent upon range of ability in group tested.		Usually not known.	Compares favorably with standard tests.	May encourage piece-meal study. Adequate criteria usually lacking.
2. Reliability	For best tests, fairly high—often .85 or more for comparable forms.	High reliability is no guarantee of validity. Also, reliability depends upon range of ability in group tested.		Reliability usually quite low.	Sometimes approaches that of standard tests.	No guarantee of validity.
3. Usability						
a. Ease of Administration	Definite procedure, time limits, etc. Economy of time.	Manuals require careful study and are sometimes inadequate.	Easy to prepare. Easy to give.	Lack of uniformity.	Directions rather uniform. Economy of time.	Time, effort, and skill are required to prepare well.
b. Ease of Scoring	Definite rules, keys, etc. Largely routine.	Scoring by hand may take considerable time and be monotonous. Machine scoring preferable.		Slow, uncertain, and subjective.	Definite rules, keys, etc. Largely routine. Can be done by clerks or machine.	Monotonous.
c. Ease of Interpretation	Better tests have adequate norms. Useful basis of comparison. Equivalent forms.	Norms often confused with standards. Some norms defective. Norms for various types of schools and levels of ability are often lacking.		No norms. Meaning doubtful.	Local norms can be derived.	No norms available at beginning.
Summary	Convenience, comparability, objectivity. Equivalent forms may be available.	Inflexibility. May be only slightly applicable to a particular situation.	Useful for part of many tests and in a few special fields.	Limited sampling. Subjective scoring. Time consuming.	Extensive sampling. Objective scoring. Flexibility.	Preparation requires skill and time.

From J. C. Stanley, Measurement in Today's Schools (Englewood Cliffs, New Jersey: Prentice-Hall, Inc., 1964). Reproduced with permission.

TABLE XII

A SUGGESTED STANDARDIZED TESTING PROGRAM FOR GRADES K-12

Type	Purpose	When Given
Reading Readiness	To determine readiness and maturity for beginning reading and to assist in establishing reading groups	End of kindergarten or beginning of first grade
Reading Achievement	To determine growth in beginning reading and diagnosis of reading difficulties	End of first and second grade
Battery of Achievement	To determine growth in basic skills, including reading, mathematics, and language. Also, for diagnosis of learning difficulties and planning remedial programs	Grades 3-8
Mental Maturity	To provide information on the nature and structure of abilities for guiding learning activities	Grades 1-4-7 or 2-5-8, depending on organization of school
Placement Tests English Mathematics	To assist in placement of students in basic freshman subjects	At the end of eighth grade or beginning of ninth grade
Battery of Achievement	To determine growth in basic subjects	Grades 9 and 11, or 10 and 12
Mental Maturity or Scholastic Aptitude Tests	To provide information on the nature and structure of abilities and aptitude for academic subjects	Grades 9 and 11, or 10 and 12
Battery of Aptitude Tests	To determine abilities in specific fields for educational and vocational guidance	Grades 11 or 12

TABLE XII (Cont'd.)

Type	Purpose	When Given
Interest Inventory	To determine the likes and dislikes of a student for educational and vocational guidance	General inventory in ninth grade and more specific interest inventory at junior level
Personality Inventory	To provide information on personal-social development for educational and vocational guidance	Grades 9 and 11

TABLE XIII

A SUGGESTED MINIMAL TESTING PROGRAM

Grade Level	Intelligence (Given in Fall)	Achievement & Diagnostic (Given in Fall or Spring)	Aptitude	Interest and Personality
K-First	Reading	Reading		
Second	Group Intelligence	Reading		
Third		Skills Battery		
Fourth	Group Intelligence	Achievement Battery Reading Diagnostic		
Fifth		Arithmetic Diagnostic		
Sixth	Group Intelligence	Achievement Battery		
Seventh		Study Skills		Problem Checklist
Eighth	Group Intelligence	Achievement Battery		
Ninth			Aptitude Battery	
Tenth	Group Intelligence*	Achievement Battery		Interest
Eleventh		Scholastic Aptitude		
Twelfth	Group Intelligence**	Achievement Battery		Interest

*Might be administered in the ninth grade if there is an 8-4 grade arrangement or if records of elementary testing are incomplete.
**For a minimum testing program, three group intelligence tests would be adequate--one in lower grades, one in intermediate grades, and one at secondary level. If the Differential Apptitude Test is used in the secondary school, it could be used to give both aptitude and intelligence scores.

From A. J. Lien, Measurement and Evaluation of Learning (Dubuque, Iowa: William C. Brown Co., 1971). Used with permission.

1. Know precisely the purposes for which the test will be used.

2. Study reference sources (textbooks, catalogs, journal reviews) to learn what tests are available in the general areas for which they are to be used.

3. Obtain copies or specimen sets of tests (all possible along with their manuals and descriptive materials).

4. Establish committees to review and criticize each test. Each test should be examined for:

   a. Its validity - the extent to which a test measures what it is supposed to measure. Any one or more of four types of validity may be cited: content, concurrent, predictive, or construct. The type of validity evidence required depends upon the purpose of the test.

   b. Its reliability - the extent to which the test is consistent in measuring what it measures. As with validity, one or more of three types of reliability coefficients may be cited: coefficient of equivalence, coefficient of internal consistency, and or coefficient of stability. Each type gives a different view of reliability, and judgment as to adequacy again rests upon the use to which the test is to be put.

   c. Suitability of norms - a comparison group to which test performance of others may be related and described. The characteristics of a test's norm population should be defined and the adequacy of the sample (basis for sampling) should be examined for their similarity to the population being tested.

   d. Its standard error of measurement - the estimate of the size of the error of measurement in a score. All test scores contain error to a certain extent. The standard error of measurement provides an estimate of the amount of error present.

   e. Practicality - whether its suitable or fits into the program because of costs, time limits, ease of marking and scoring, and availability of suitable interpretative aids. (pp. 213-214)

In order to select the best test available for the desired purpose, many test evaluation procedures are available. Harrington (1969) suggests a form (Figure 15) which will enable those in charge of selecting standardized tests to compile information on several tests concurrently. When this information is available on several tests being evaluated, the decision as to which test to finally suggest is made much easier.

TEST ADMINISTRATION PROCEDURES

Some general suggestions for standardized test administration are suggested by Lindeman (1967) and apply regardless of who the examiner may be:

1. The examiner should familiarize himself thoroughly with the test directions prior to administration. Reading them aloud to another person is helpful in providing such familiarity. The directions should be read exactly as they appear in the "Directions for Administering" section of the test manual.

2. Every effort should be made to ensure that students understand exactly what is to be done. If students ask questions prior to the test, they should be answered. After the test begins, questions should be discouraged, but the examiner should circulate around the room to see that everyone is working on the correct page and is marking his answers in the proper manner.

3. During the test, students should be comfortable, relaxed, and free from interruptions and distractions. Particularly for young children, it is best if testing takes place in the regular classroom. Temperature and lighting conditions should be properly controlled.

4. Time limits should be observed exactly. A departure of even 5 or 10 per cent can destroy the comparability of results.

5. When the test is completed, the examiner should check all papers as they are collected to see that identifying information, such as name, age, class, and date, is entered properly on each test.

6. All necessary steps should be taken to ensure that

Directions: Complete each statement by circling or filling in the best response unless specific directions are given.

Evaluator _____

Name of Test _____

Author(s) _____

Publisher _____ Copyright _____

Level: Of the Test Grade _____ Age(s) _____

Type of Test (Mental, achievement, etc.) _____

I.   Cost: (Use prices as listed in Buros, Noll, or the test company catalog.)
     A. Financial
        1. Unit cost $ _____ per _____
        2. Answer sheets cost _____ (if separate)
        3. Is the test booklet reusable?   yes _____   no _____
     B. Time
        1. The time of administration is _____ hours _____ minutes
        2. Can the test be administered in parts? yes _____ no _____
     C. Equivalent Forms
        1. Number _____

II. Objectivity: The degree to which the examiner's judgment is eliminated. Comments to be completed only when any of the following items tend to be subjective.
     A. The directions for administration

     B. The scoring

     C. Interpretation of test results

III. Standardization
     A. Describe the standardization group. (Size, age, area, etc.)

     B. Validity: The degree to which the test measures what it is designed to measure.
        1. The coefficient of validity is: (Please use the lowest index given.)
           a. Insufficient   b. adequate   c. high   d. not given
              (below .40)   (.40 to .70)   (above .70)
        2. Indicate how validity was determined if the coefficient was not given.

Figure 15.   Test Evaluation Form

134

3. Comments by the evaluator on the validity (optional).

C. Reliability: The degree to which the test results are consistent.
   1. The coefficient of reliability is: (Please use the lowest index given.)
      a. insufficient   b. adequate   c. high   d. not given
      (0-.70)   (.70-.90)   (above .90)
   2. The coefficient of reliability was determined in what manner.
      a. Test   b. Equivalent   c. Odds   d. Split   e. Kuder   f. Other
      Re-test   Forms   Evens   Half   Richardson
   3. Was the Spearman-Brown prophecy formula used? yes _____
                                              no _____
   4. Comments by the evaluator on reliability (optional)
D. Norms
   Types of norms given (percentile, age, grade, etc.)

IV.   Test Manual: A complete manual contains all of the preceding information with the following additions.

   A. List the advantages and purposes of the test.

   B. List the suggestions for use of the test.

V.   Mental Measurements Yearbook: To gain other opinions of the test please review the mental measurements yearbook by Oscar Buros.

   A. List advantages of the test.

   B. List disadvantages of the test.

VI.   What are your opinions of the test?

From W. E. Harrington, A Study Guide for Measurement (Dubuque, Iowa: William C. Brown Publishers, 1969). Reproduced with permission.

scoring is done accurately. Ideally, all tests shoul
be rescored by a different person before the scores
are recorded on cumulative record cards.

7. Be sure that all pertinent data about the test are
recorded on the pupil's record card, including the
name of the test, names and scores on subtests, and
the date of administration.

8. Arrange special testing sessions for pupils who
were absent on the regular testing date. These
sessions should be held as soon as possible after
the regular session so that results for all pupils
will be comparable. (p. 111)

GUIDES IN STANDARDIZED TESTING

Traxler (1962) has summarized some suggestions or
guidelines which should be observed in organizing, imple-
menting, and using standardized tests:

1. Make sure that all tests are administered under
favorable working conditions and with faithful
attention to the manual of directions. The best
tests will give useless results if they are not
administered well.

2. Carefully plan and carry out the scoring procedure,
or utilize outside professional scoring services,
to insure accuracy and reasonable dispatch.

3. Report the results promptly, with appropriate interpretations, to guidance personnel and teacher, and
have the scores and percentiles recorded on cumulative records.

4. Make the test results available to parents who are
willing to come to the school for interviews. Do
not release the scores to parents in routine fashion
by mail.

5. Express the results of scholastic aptitude tests in
percentiles or other easily understood terms. Except
in rare instances, avoid the use of I.Q.'s.

6. Disregard small differences between pupils in score
on a test and for the same pupil on different kinds o
tests.

7. Relate test results to other kinds of information about the pupil. Do not depend exclusively on test scores and never regard the results of just one test as final.

8. Make sure that you understand the data yielded by a test before you try to interpret them for yourself or others.

9. Pay attention to the past test results for an individual pupil; that is, to his cumulative record. Growth is often more important than status.

10. See that the teachers in your school have continuous opportunity to become well informed concerning the meaning and interpretation of the results of the tests. (pp. 219-220)

BRIEF DESCRIPTIONS OF REPRESENTATIVE STANDARDIZED TESTS
(Thorndike and Hagen, 1969)*

ELEMENTARY-SCHOOL ACHIEVEMENT BATTERIES

Comprehensive Tests of Basic Skills (CTBS)

California Test Bureau   Testing time: 240-260 min.
Range: Grades 2.5-4.9; 4.0-6.9; 6.0-8.9

The CTBS is the 1968 revision of the California Achievement Tests. The battery consists of 10 subtests: (1) reading vocabulary, (2) reading comprehension, (3) language mechanics, (4) language expression, (5) language spelling, (6) arithmetic computation, (7) arithmetic concepts, (8) arithmetic applications, (9) study skills using reference materials, and (10) study skills using graphic materials. The battery yields 15 scores, one for each of the 10 subtests, a total for each skill area, and a total battery score. The tests were normed with the California Short-Form Test of Mental Maturity. Except for tables of norms, description of normative sample, and analysis of content of each subtest, no technical data were

---

*From Robert L. Thorndike and Elizabeth Hagen, Measurement and Evaluation in Psychology and Education (New York: John Wiley &Sons, Inc., 3rd Edition, 1969) pp. 664-690. Used with permission.

available in January 1969. The absence of any reliability
data in the manual for examiners and test coordinators is
particularly troublesome. An examination of the normative
tables indicates that each level of the test appears to be
too difficult for the first grade of the level and too easy
for the last grade of the level; for example, the level for
grades 2.5-4.9 appears to be too difficult for the last half
of grade 2 and too easy for the last half of grade 4. The
subtests appear to be too short to appraise adequately the
range of achievement that each is supposed to cover.

Iowa Tests of Basic Skills (ITBS)

Houghton Mifflin Company   Testing time: 280-335 min.
Range: Grades 3-9

    The ITBS uses a multilevel format, with a single spiral-
bound reusable test booklet for all grades. Test level is
controlled by starting and stopping at different points. The
battery yields 15 scores: vocabulary (one score), reading
comprehension (one score), language (for subscores and one
total score), work-study skills (three subscores and one total
score), arithmetic skills (two subscores and one total score),
and composite score. The battery emphasizes the appraisal of
functional skills needed by the child if he is to make progress in school. Reliabilities of the subtests are adequate
and, of the total tests, are high. Procedures for norming
the test were excellent. The ITBS and the Lorge-Thorndike
Intelligence Tests were normed simultaneously and percentile
norms by intelligence level are provided in a supplementary
manual. In addition to general national norms, special
percentile norms are provided for building averages, geographical region, large cities, and Catholic schools. The manuals
are excellent - particularly the ones for the teacher and for
the administrator. A modern mathematics supplement is available for use in addition to or to replace the arithmetic
skills tests in the regular battery.

Metropolitan Achievement Test, 1959 Edition

Harcourt, Brace & World, Inc.
Range: Primary I, grades 1.5-2.5   Testing time: 95-100 min.
       Primary II, grades 2-3.5   105-115 min.
       Elementary, grades 3-4   160-175 min.
       Intermediate, grades 5-6   250-280 min.
       Advanced, grades 7-8   260-290 min.

All of the batteries measure vocabulary, reading comprehension, and arithmetic skills. Word discrimination is tested in the three lowest levels; spelling begins in the Primary II battery and continues through the other levels. Language skills are added in the Elementary battery and continue through the other batteries. Language study skills, social studies information, social studies study skills, and science are parts of the intermediate and advanced batteries. The format of all the tests is attractive. Test content in the skills area appears to be adequate, and the test items, on the whole, are well written. Norming procedures are good. Reliabilities of total scores for all tests are adequate. A revised form of the Metropolitan is scheduled to be published for use in the fall of 1970.

SRA Achievement Series, 1964 Edition

Science Research Associates
Range: Grades 1-2   Testing time: 270-300 min.
       Grades 2-4   300-360 min.
       Grades 4-9   420-450 min.

The levels of the test designed for use in grades 1-2 and grades 2-4 are published as separate batteries; the one designed for grades 4-9 is published in a multilevel format. Reading and arithmetic skills are appraised at all levels; a subtest in language arts is added at grades 2-4 and all higher levels; and subtests in social studies and science are added at grades 4 and above. A test of work-study skills is provided as a supplement at grades 4 and above. The tests are very attractive and make good use of color. In the multilevel battery, answer sheets for different grades are color coded. The tests in science and social studies tend to emphasize recall of factual information. Vocabulary is appraised only in context of a reading selection. Reliability coefficients (K-R #20) are satisfactory but may be somewhat inflated. Grade equivalent, percentile, and stanine norms are provided at all grade levels. Procedures for norming, establishing the content of the tests, and determining reliability are inadequately reported.

Stanford Achievement Tests, 1964 Revision

Harcourt, Brace & World
Range: Grades 1.5-2.4   Testing time: 160-170 min.
          Grades 2.5-3.9   230-250 min.
          Grades 4.0-5.4   230-300 min.
          Grades 5.5-6.9   220-300 min.
          Grades 7.0-9.9   200-285 min.

The subtests included at each level vary, but reading, spelling, and arithmetic are included at all levels. At grade 4 and above, the battery can be purchased as a partial battery or complete battery. The complete battery includes subtests in social studies and science. Split-half and K-R #20 reliability coefficients are given and these tend to be satisfactory at all levels. No equivalent form reliabilities are given. Grade equivalent, percentile, and stanine norms are provided. Norms by stanine levels of performance on the Otis Quick-Scoring Mental Ability Test are given in the Technical Report and in the manual for administering the tests.

HIGH SCHOOL ACHIEVEMENT BATTERIES

Comprehensive Tests of Basic Skills (CTBS)

California Test Bureau   Testing time: 240-260 min.
Range: 8.0-12.9

This is the highest level of the same battery described in Section D. The range of grades to be covered by this level appears to be too large for a single, relatively short battery of tests. No reliability or other technical data were available for the tests early in 1969.

Iowa Tests of Educational Development (ITED)

Science Research Associates   Testing time: 330-540 min.
Range: Grades 9-12

The battery consists of 9 subtests: (1) understanding of basic social concepts, (2) general background in the natural sciences, (3) correctness and appropriateness of expression, (4) ability to do quantitative thinking, (5) ability to interpret reading materials in the social studies, (6) ability to interpret reading materials in the natural sciences, (7) ability to interpret literary materials, (8) general vocabulary, and (9) uses of sources of information. The battery yields 10 scores, one for each subtest and a composite total score based on the first 8 subtests. Predictive validity data and concurrent validity data are provided. Correlations between composite scores obtained in grades 10, 11, or 12 and grades in the freshman year of college range from .40 to .71 with a median of approximately .60. Internal consistency reliabilities are satisfactory. Correlations among subtests tend to be high in the .70's; therefore, the value of the tests as a diagnostic instrument is questionable. Standard scores, percentiles, and percentile bands are provided.

Metropolitan Achievement Tests: High School Battery (MAT)

Harcourt, Brace & World   Testing time: 315-330 min.
Range: Grades 9-13

The battery consists of 11 subtests: (1) reading, (2) spelling, (3) language arts, (4) language study skills, (5) social studies skills, (6) social studies vocabulary, (7) social studies information, (8) mathematical computation and concepts, (9) mathematical analysis and problem solving, (10) scientific concepts and understandings, and (11) science information. The language, mathematics, science, and social studies subtests are available as separate tests. Alternate form reliability coefficients (time interval not specified) for grades 10 and 11 combined range from .72 to .90 with a median of approximately .84. Split-half reliabilities for grades 10 and 11 combined are slightly higher with a median coefficient of about .86. Internal consistency reliabilities (K-R #20) for a single grade tend to cluster between .82 and .88. Percentile and stanine norms are provided for age-controlled smaples at each grade level and for college preparatory groups at each grade level. Tables are also provided for comparing performance on the achievement tests with students who performed at different levels on the Otis Quick-Scoring Mental Ability Tests: Gamma.

Tests of Academic Progress (TAP)

Houghton Mifflin Company   Testing time: 330-340 min.
Range: Grades 9-12

The battery consists of four overlapping tests, one for each grade, in the following six areas: (1) social studies, (2) composition, (3) science, (4) reading, (5) mathematics, and (6) literature. The tests are available in a single booklet or as separate booklets. Three types of norms are provided: standard score norms, grade-percentile norms for individual students, and grade-percentile norms for school averages. The tests were standardized in a coordinated program with the Iowa

Tests of Basic Skills and the Lorge-Thorndike Intelligence Test Split-half reliability coefficients for the different grades are .85 or better except for the science subtest at grade 9 for which it is .83. The majority of the reliability coefficients are .89 or better. Standard errors of measurement are given for each subtest and for each grade for total score and at selected percentile-rank levels. TAP is a well-constructed, well-normed battery of tests that should be useful in a wide variety of secondary schools.

GENERAL INTELLIGENCE TESTS (MENTAL ABILITY)

California Short Form Test of Mental Maturity, 1963 Revision (CTMM)

California Test Bureau   Testing time: 40-45 min.
Range: Kindergarten-1.5,
       Grades 1-3, 3-4, 4-5, 6-7, 7-9, 9-12, 12-16

The CTMM yields three scores: (1) language IQ, (2) non-language IQ, and (3) total IQ. Only one form of the test is available at each level. Some information is given in this edition of the nature of the factor scores. However, the factor scores are based on a relatively small number of items. The reliability of the nonlanguage subtest tends to be low. The artwork in the nonlanguage section is poor. The language portion of the test has a heavy emphasis on vocabulary. Predictive validity data are not given in the technical supplement but the language IQ should have adequate correlations with academic achievement for the higher grades.

Cooperative School and College Ability Tests (SCAT)

Cooperative Test Division   Testing time: 60-75 min.
Educational Testing Service
Range: Grades 4-6, 6-8, 8-10, 10-12, 12-14

SCAT yields three scores: (1) verbal, (2) quantitative, and (3) total. Manuals and interpretative materials accompanying the tests are excellent. Reliability coefficients are reported for only one form. The total score correlates well with measures of school success, but there is little evidence for differential prediction from the verbal and quantitative scores. Percentile and standard score norms are provided.

Henmon-Nelson Tests of Mental Ability, Revised Edition

Houghton Mifflin Company   Testing time: 30-45 min.
Range: Grades 3-6, 6-9, 9-12, 13-14

The tests designed for elementary and secondary schools yield a single overall score; the college-level test yields three scores: (1) verbal, (2) quantitative, and (3) total. The total score correlates well with other group tests of intelligence, with teachers' grades and with achievement test results. Reliability coefficients estimated by use of parallel forms range from .87 to .94 for the total score. Normative data for the elementary and secondary school levels and college freshmen are good but norms are lacking for other levels of the college edition. Only percentile norms are presented for the college edition.

Kuhlmann-Anderson Intelligence Tests, Seventh Edition (K-A)

Personnel Press, Inc.   Testing time: 25-60 min.
Range: Kindergarten; 1, 2, 3-4, 4-5, 5-7, 7-9, 9-12

The K-A consists of eight subtests at all levels. The lower levels yield a single overall score; the higher levels yield three scores: (1) verbal, (2) quantitative, and (3) total. Percentile norms and standard score norms (deviation IQ's) are available for each level. Reliability coefficients are generally satisfactory. The difference score between the verbal and quantitative subtests does not appear to have high enough reliability to be used. Data on concurrent validity are satisfactory, but there are few predictive validity coefficients reported in the technical manual. The subtests have very short time limits and, therefore, place heavy demands on the examinees for fast work and on the examiner for accurate timing.

Lorge-Thorndike Intelligence Tests, Multi-Level Edition (L-T)

Houghton Mifflin Company   Testing time: 35-45 min.
Range: Grade 3 through college freshmen

For a description of the tests, see pp. 296-298. The L-T, Iowa Tests of Basic Skills, and The Tests of Academic Progress were normed together. Norming procedures were excellent. Standard scores (deviation IQ's), grade percentiles, and age equivalents are provided. Alternate form reliabilities range from .80 to .92 for the nonverbal battery with a median of .88. For the verbal battery the range is from .83 to .94 with a median of .90. Correlations of different forms given 1 to 3 years apart yield coefficients of stability from .49 for a 3-year interval and from .58 to .88 for a 1-year interval. Standard errors of measurement are provided for different score levels. Concurrent, construct, and predictive validity data are provided. Median predictive validity correlations against grades or rank in a class are approximately .56 at the high school level for the verbal battery and .65 at the elementary school level. For the nonverbal battery, correlations average about .52 for elementary school grades.

Otis-Lennon Mental Ability Tests

Harcourt, Brace & World, Inc.   Testing time: 30-50 min.
Range: Kindergarten; 1-1.5; 1.6-3-9; 4.0-6.9; 7.0-9.9; 10.0-12

This series is a revision of the Otis Quick-Scoring Mental Ability Test and closely resembles it. It has a spiral omnibus format and yields a total IQ. A very complete technical handbook is provided that describes procedures for constructing the test and gives complete data on validity, reliability, and standardization. Alternate form reliabilities with one or two week intervals range from .81 for age 5 to a high of .94 for age 14 with a median of .92. Split-half and K-R #21 reliability coefficients run slightly higher. Standard errors of measurement are reported for different score levels as well as overall. Predictive and concurrent validity data are reported and compare favorably with those reported for other instruments. Deviation IQ's, percentile norms, and mental ages are provided.

SRA Tests of Education Ability,
1962 Edition (TEA)

Science Research Associates   Testing time: 30-70 min.
Range: Grades 4-6, 6-9, 9-12

The TEA provides four scores: (1) language, (2) reasoning (3) quantitative, and (4) total, and the lowest level yields an additional score, nonreading. However, the manuals suggest that only total scores be used and the evidence on validity is primarily in terms of total scores. The predictive validity data presented in the manual are for short-term (two months or less) prediction and should be interpreted with caution. The samples used to norm the test can be questioned both as to representativeness and size. Reliability of total scores is adequate. The technical manual is poorly written and difficult to understand. Conversion of the raw scores in terms of grade placement rather than age placement makes comparison with other tests difficult.

SRA Tests of General Ability (TOGA)

Science Research Associates   Testing time: 35-45 min.
Range: Kindergarten-2, 2-4, 4-6, 6-9, 9-12

     TOGA attempts to reduce stress on school-learned skills by presenting all test items at all levels in pictorial form. One subtest at each level is supposed to appraise reasoning and the other subtest is supposed to appraise information. Normative samples at all levels are small and not representative geographically. The reasoning subtest is claimed to be "culture-fair" but no evidence is presented to support this claim. Concurrent validity data presented indicate that TOGA appraises about the same functions as other commonly used intelligence tests and ranks students approximately in the same way. Total score reliability coefficients (split-half) range from .80 to .90 with a median of .87. Directions for administering the test are clear but permit the administrator of the test considerable leeway to alter timing particularly in the information test.

APTITUDE TEST BATTERIES

Academic Promise Tests (APT)

The Psychological Corporation   Testing time: 90-120 min.
Range: Grades 6-9

     The APT consists of four subtests: (1) abstract reasoning, (2) numerical, (3) verbal, and (4) language usage, which yield 4 separate subscores and 3 scores from combining the subtests. Reliability coefficients (internal consistency and parallel forms) are high. Predictive validity coefficients between test scores and grades are given. Percentile norms are provided for each grade. The tests should be useful in educational guidance and for sectioning and placing students.

The Dailey Vocational Tests

Houghton Mifflin Company   Testing time: 115-140 min.
Range: Grades 8-12 and adults

     This battery, designed for noncollege-bound students, consists of three tests: the Technical and Scholastic Test, yielding seven subscores, a technical and scholastic score and a total score; the Spatial Visualization Test, and the Business English Test. Subtest scores of the Technical and Scholastic Test are quite short and unreliable. Normative data are incomplete and somewhat confusing. Validity data are

largely limited to differences between high school curricular
groups. Tests for students not headed for college are needed,
but more information is required on this battery before it can
be recommended for use.

Multiple Aptitude Tests (MAT)

California Test Bureau   Testing time: 175-220 min.
Range: Grades 7-13

The battery consists of nine tests providing nine separate
scores, which in turn yield scores on four basic factors. The
word meaning, language usage, and arithmetic computation and
reasoning tests have reliabilities in the high .80's or low .90's
and are quite satisfactory; but the reliabilities for paragraph
meaning, applied science and mechanics, and spatial relations
tend to be only in the high .70's and this makes them somewhat
less useful for individual guidance. Predictive validity data
for school marks are given and tend to be disappointingly
low. Concurrent validity for 42 different occupational groups
is given showing differences in occupational profiles on the
tests; however, these were obtained for groups that were
already engaged in the occupation.

SRA Primary Mental Abilities, Revised (PMS)

Science Research Associates   Testing time: 65-75 min. (2-4)
Range: Kindergarten-1   50-107 min. (4-6)
        Grades 2-4, 4-6, 6-9, 9-12   35-75 min. (6-9,
                                                             9-12)

Although this instrument, yielding 4 subscores as well as
a total score (except in the form for grades 4-6, which yields
5 subscores), is promoted in terms of the differential information provided by the part scores, evidence of differential
validity is scanty and most data are for the total score.
Only one form is available, and for this test-retest reliabilities of total score are in the .80's or low .90's. Data
on subtest validities, reliabilities, and norms are meager.

146

California Psychological Inventory (CPI)

Consulting Psychologists Press, Inc.   Testing time: 45-60 min.
Range: Grades 13 and over

The CPI has been developed for use with normal populations.
It consists of 480 items to be answered "true or false." About
one-half of the items on the CPI have been taken from the MMPI.
The CPI yields 18 scores, three of which are check scales to
determine test-taking attitudes. Items on 11 of the 15 scales
were selected on their ability to discriminate contrasting
groups. Test-retest reliabilities for high school groups over
a year interval averaged .65 for males and .68 for females.
Retest reliabilities for an adult group over a one- to three-
week interval averaged about .80. Intercorrelations among
the scores tend to be high, indicating that the scores are not
as independent as the manual tends to imply. Separate norms
are provided by sex for high school and college samples. Some
of the validity data based on differences between extreme groups
are questionable.

California Test of Personality, 1953 Revision

California Test Bureau   Testing time: 45-60 min.
Range: Kindergarten to grade 3;
         grades 4 to 8, 7 to 10, 9 to 16; adults

This is one of the few personality inventories that have
forms for use in the elementary school. Evidence on the
validity of the scales is scanty. Reliability data indicate
that only the total score and its two components, social and
personal, are stable enough to use. The "right" answer to
many of the questions seems obvious. At the elementary levels,
the inventories require at least an average reading ability,
limiting its usefulness with the low-achieving child. Suggestions given in the test manual for the use of the test
results are questionable at best. In the hands of a person
untrained in psychology, the suggestions could have disastrous
consequences.

147

The IPAT Anxiety Scale

Institute for Personality and Ability Testing

Testing time: 5-10 min.

Range: Ages 14 and over

The Scale consists of 40 items that yield five part scores and a total score. In addition, the 40 items yield separate "covert" and "overt" anxiety scores. Construction of the Anxiety Scale was based on extensive factor analytic studies. The validity of the Scale is based on the factor analytic studies and external criteria. External validity is based on correlations of total scores with psychiatric ratings (range .30 to .40 uncorrected for attenuation); differences in mean scores between anxiety neurotics and the standardization population; and differences in mean scores among other clinically diagnosed groups.

Reliability coefficients for the part scores, based on subtests with as few as four items and a maximum of 12 items, are too low to justify the use of part scores with individuals. The Scale is probably most useful as a quick screening device for literate adults and as a research instrument.

Mooney Problem Check List

The Psychological Corporation

Testing time: 20-40 min.

Range: Forms for grades 7-9, 9-12, 13-16, and adults

These check lists provide a systematic coverage of problems often reported or judged significant at the different age levels. Though the items are grouped by areas (health and physical development; courtship, sex, and marriage; home and family; etc.) and a count can be made of items marked in each area, emphasis is placed on using the individual responses as leads and openings for an interview. This instrument does not claim to be a test and the use proposed for it is the type that is probably most justifiable for a self-report instrument.

INTEREST INVENTORIES

Brainard Occupational Preference Inventory

The Psychological Corporation

Testing time: 30 min.

Range: Grades 8-12; adults

The inventory covers six broad occupational fields: (1) commercial, (2) mechanical, (3) professional, (4) aesthetic, (5) scientific, and (6) personal service (for girls) or

agriculture (for boys). Each occupational field is covered
by twenty items which the respondent marks on a five-point
scale ranging from "like very much" to "dislike very much."
Data in the manual show that the instrument has moderate to
low correlations with the Kuder Preference Record-Vocational.
Scoring is simple. Evidence on validity is lacking.

Gordon Occupational Check List (OCL)

Harcourt, Brace & World   Testing time: 20-25 min.
Range: High school students not planning
       to enter college

The OCL is designed for use with individuals who have a
high school education or less. The inventory contains 240
statements of job duties and tasks that are found in occupations at the middle and lower levels of skill and
responsibility. The statements are classified into five broad
occupational groupings. Top-level managerial and professional
occupations are not included. Test-retest reliability data
tend to be in the middle or high .80's. No norms are reported.
Validity data are meager.

Kuder Preference Record-Occupational

Science Research Associates, Inc.   Testing time: 25-35 min.
Range: Grades 9-16 and adults

The KPR-Occupational yields 50 scores for specific
occupational groups and one verification score. The occupational keys were developed by comparing answers of men in
specific occupations with men in general. Concurrent validity
data only are reported in the manual. No predictive validity
are provided. Test-retest reliability data are scarce. The
only test-retest data reported in the manual are over a one-
month interval; the median correlation is .85. Correlation is
.85. Correlations between Kuder scales and the corresponding
scale of the Strong Vocational Interest Blank tend to be low
to moderate. At the present time, more data on reliability and
validity are needed.

Kuder Preference Record-Personal

Science Research Associates   Testing time: 40-45 min.
Range: Grade 9-16 and adults

    Using the same pattern for items as the Kuder Preference Record-Vocational, this inventory appraises liking for five more aspects of life situations; being active in groups, being in familiar and stable situations, working with ideas, avoiding conflict, and directing others. The scores are fairly independent of each other and of those in the Vocational blank. The value of these scales for guidance purposes is less fully explored than that of the scales in the Vocational form.

Chapter VIII

OTHER INDICES OF PUPIL PROGRESS:
OBSERVATIONAL TESTS

In evaluating the progress of pupils, the classroom teacher should have in his repertoire skills in using subjective measures as well as objective measures. Previous chapters have emphasized objective or formal types of tests such as the classroom teacher-made test and standardized tests. This chapter focuses on subjective or informal types of measures, observations, which can be important adjuncts to either teacher-made or standardized tests.

OBSERVATION

Observational tools are subjective or informal measures or instruments of interpretation which may yield qualitative or descriptive results which may be used in studying pupils. Observations should be considered as important supplements to other methods and techniques for evaluating pupil progress and growth.

Observational measures differ from typical paper-and-pencil tests in two ways. First, they are normally used on only one student at a time. Second, when using observational tools, the teacher normally does the recording.

Opportunities for Observing Pupils

Gibson and Higgins (1966) suggest that the opportunities for observing students are diverse and ever present in any school, whether the small elementary school or the complex college campus. They then suggest six observation opportunities in the school:

1. The Classroom. Each subject-matter classroom experience offers distinctive opportunities for pupil observation. The pupil's interest and aptitude in the subject, his adjustment to various kinds of classroom exercises, his behavior in the structured group and subgroup situations of the classroom, and his reactions to success and failure are among the characteristics that may be noted.

2. The Playground and Recreation Areas. The school playground and recreation areas provide opportunities to observe a different side of the student. Here,

with supervision at a minimum and associations and activities usually voluntary and informal, different kinds of interests, skills, and relationships as well as behavior patterns may be observed. Sportsmanship, leadership, peer group associations, consideration of others, sense of humor., and physical well-being and coordination are among the observable characteristics.

3. The Gymnasium. Physical education and gymnasium activities lie somewhere between the permissiveness of the playground and the structured routine of the classroom. Physical education activities offer prime situations for observing the development of certain motor skills, interest and competitiveness in group and individual games, sportsmanship, effort as a team member, and skill as a team leader. In addition one may note a pupil's regard for the rules of the game, self-discipline, reactions to victory and defeat, personal health habits, and peer associations.

4. School Cafeteria or Dining Halls. The school cafeteria and collegiate dining halls can provide opportunities for observations of the student's eating habits, diet, manners, personal health habits, and patterns of peer associations.

5. School Activities. The various school activities can provide opportunities to observe the student as he participates in social events, hobbies or projects of special interest, clubs and student government, and areas of special skill, such as dramatics, music, or art. These activities are especially significant because the student usually engages in them by choice.

6. The Homeroom. The pupil's homeroom is in a sense his "home away from home." If the homeroom group is relatively stable for several years, excellent opportunities are available to observe over a period of time for roles and relationships, behavior patterns, and developmental trends. The homeroom is usually free of the tensions and pressures of the subject-matter classroom, and may therefore provide a more relaxed and informal atmosphere in which to observe. (pp. 106-107)

152

Values of Observation

Because observational tools tend to be highly subjective in nature, teachers often avoid using these methods. They may be mislead in thinking that unless an instrument is highly objective, it has little or no use in measuring and evaluating pupil progress. There are times when observations may be more appropriate than objective type instruments. Michaels and Karnes suggest five uses and advantages of observation:

1. Observation of the student's daily work as he applies principles and procedures provides a continuous check on the student's daily achievement. Observation provides an incentive for the student to show growth toward goals, and it enables the teacher to note errors as they occur.

2. Observation provides a check on certain important outcomes of instruction without encroaching on instructional time or disrupting training in any way.

3. If observation can be made reliable and objective, the results, more than that of any other measure, should be a valid indication of the student's ability to use and apply what has been taught. In Chapter 2, the three levels of measurement and evaluation were described. In order of preference, these were behavioral, planning, and understanding. Observational tools are an example of the behavioral level of evaluation, since they are a direct measure of the student's performance.

4. The time, equipment, and personnel required to administer carefully controlled performance tests make extensive use of them impractical. Observational tools can be used as a very effective supplement to a few carefully prepared performance tests and written examinations.

5. Observational tools have wide applicability to non-academic growth (cooperation, consideration, initiative, enthusiasm, and the like) as well as to subject matter growth. (pp. 371-372)

Gibson and Higgins (1966) suggest that in planning the utilization of observational techniques, the contributions they can make should be determined. They list the potential values of observation:

1. **Directs attention to pupils as individuals.**
   Effective observation demands the concentration of
   attention on the individual so that the observer
   can become acquainted with his unique characteristics.

2. **Promotes better understanding of the pupil.**
   The more the pupil is observed as a unique individual,
   the better the observer is able to understand him and
   his behavior.

3. **Promotes teacher-pupil relationships.**
   The insights into pupil behavior that a teacher gains
   through observation help him in developing positive
   relationships with pupils.

4. **Contributes to instructional effectiveness.**
   Instructional methods and materials can be more
   effectively adapted to pupil needs, interests, and
   capacities through the application of the understanding
   gained through observation.

5. **Promotes identification of talent.**
   Observation helps identify pupils with special
   abilities. Each classroom teacher has an opportunity
   to observe for those pupils having talents or skills
   related to a particular subject-matter area.

6. **Aids in identifying pupils who need assistance.**
   Directed observation of pupils can often identify those
   in need of teacher or counselor assistance. Since
   many such persons do not engage in conspicuous
   behavior calling attention to their problem, they are
   liable to go unnoticed and unassisted until their
   problem emerges at a more serious level. Planned
   observation can lead to early detection of such
   problems or adjustment needs.

7. **Contributes to the general pool of knowledge about the
   individual pupil.**
   Observation is one of several means of gathering
   general information about the pupil. This information
   becomes more meaningful, as does information collected
   by other techniques, when pooled with all available
   records for pupil analysis.

8. **Provides clues for more effective counseling.**
   The counselor may find that teacher and other staff
   observations provide useful clues for counseling the
   individual. Practically all the values of observation

contribute to the effectiveness of general pupil counseling; observations of a pupil can also provide clues directly related to his individual counseling on specific problems.

9. Assists the pupil in seeing himself as others see him. When a counselor interprets pupil data, including observation reports, to the pupil himself, he helps the pupil gain a better understanding of how others see him. Too, the very knowledge that he is noticed as an individual may stimulate the pupil to self-improvement.

10. Promotes more effective future observations. The more often one engages in purposeful and directed observation, the more skillful one becomes in utilizing this technique. Experienced observers become more conscious of details, nonverbal communications, subtleties of group dynamics, and a host of other clues. This increased sensitivity enhances individual analysis. (pp. 107-108)

Improving Observations

The ability to make good observations is probably a function of practice and experience. Practice in which two or more individuals observe simultaneously and compare results will help to develop these skills. Shertzer and Stone (1971) list other considerations which help control the observer's techniques:

1. Before observation takes place, determine what is to be observed. The purpose of the observation should be known in advance. What dimensions of behavior are to be looked for? What traits are to be investigated? Knowing these things will add meaning and purpose to observation periods.

2. Observe only one pupil at a time. Few well-trained observers can watch with any degree of accuracy two or more pupils at one time. When group behavior is studied, film and recording equipment should be used to obtain a record of the multitude of happenings that take place simultaneously.

3. Watch for significant behavior. Just what is significant may not be entirely clear at the time it occurs just as many of the things a pupil does are trivial and reveal nothing about him.

4. Spread observations over the school day. Time sampling of behavior, i.e., observing a pupil at 8:00, 10:30, 12:00, 1:00, etc., for brief periods of time often gives a truer, more comprehensive description of his behavior than does a description obtained from a few prolonged observations.

5. Learn to observe without resorting to writing notes during the observation period. The presence of a pad and pencil often cues children regarding what is occurring and results in behavior different from what might be obtained if these were absent. Significant behavior will probably be remembered anyway.

6. If possible, record and summarize the observation immediately after it is completed. (pp. 272-273)

Gibson and Higgins (1966) list nine principles which must be considered of critical importance to any person being observed:

1. Observe one student at a time.
   If an observation report is to be used for individual analysis, it is essential that the observer concentrate on the individual. This does not mean that the observer disregards all others in a group or the individual's relation to them, but it does mean that he concentrates on and directs his primary attention to a single pupil for whatever length of time is necessary to make an accurate and meaningful observation.

2. Observe the student in the context of the total situation.
   As has been indicated, the observer cannot ignore a student's relation to a group and his role in group activity, for the social context may contribute heavily to his observable characteristics. As an extreme example, observing and reporting the appearance of Joe Jones after the annual freshman-sophomore mud-bowl fight hardly qualifies as fair for a strict and final accounting of Joe's appearance. Any observation report can be somewhat misleading unless the observer notes and reports the circumstances in which this observation was made.

3. The student should be observed over a period of time.
   Because everyone has days when he is not at his best and days when he performs unusually well, to draw

conclusions from a single observation is to assume that the observer has, with uncanny accuracy, picked the most appropriate moment to note the student's most typical behavior. The validity of analysis by observation increases with the number of observations and the length of time over which the observations have been made. Too, observing over a considerable period of time is valuable in identifying changes in pupil characteristics and recognizing developmental trends.

4. The student should be observed in a number of different situations.
Here again, if the observer is to get a complete and accurate picture of the individual, observations cannot be limited to one type of situation on the assumption that it is typical. The teacher and the parent may reach an impasse because the teacher observes Johnny as a demon in the classroom and the parent observes Johnny as Lord Fauntleroy at home. Perhaps each is correct in the observations he is reporting, but neither has a complete picture of Johnny because his observations are limited to a single setting.

In developing as complete a picture of the individual as possible, a pupil should be observed in each of the varied school settings described earlier. In addition, occasional opportunities may arise to obtain the observations of people outside the school who have observed the pupil in the context of the home, a part-time job, church activities, and neighborhood play groups.

5. Have specific criteria for making observations.
Observation techniques should be employed when they can serve a definite purpose. Specific criteria may then be established that reflect this purpose. For example, if students are to be observed for the purpose of selecting one for a good-citizenship award, observations would be directed toward specific behavior designated as representative of good citizenship.

6. Observations must be conducted from a vantage point that enables the observer to see clearly what he is planning to report.
Anyone who has found himself sitting behind a grandstand post at the ball park will understand the elementary importance of a clear field of vision for

accuracy in observation. It makes no less sense to
have a broadcaster observe and report the game from
that seat behind the post than for a teacher or
guidance worker to report on student behavior in
circumstances that deny a clear view. Since the
school does offer many excellent opportunities for
unobscured observations, reports based on partial
viewings should be strongly discouraged. Considering
the inherent limitations of observation under the
best of circumstances, an observer cannot afford the
further handicap of obstructed vision.

7. Observe without bias.
    Observations should be strictly impartial, accen-
    tuating neither the positive nor the negative in an
    individual. School personnel sometimes tend to
    report observations of a pupil's misbehavior more
    readily than his praiseworthy or neutral behavior;
    however, finding fault is not the purpose of obser-
    vation. Neither should observation reports be used
    to bolster the record of one's favorite student;
    that is simply another form of bias. Observation
    that is slanted (whether through misunderstanding
    or intentionally) toward either the negative or
    positive qualities of the individual is unacceptable,
    for it defeats the basic value of the technique -
    provision of a fair record of all kinds of pupil
    behavior that may yield significant insights.

8. Be interested and attentive in planned observations.
    If observations are to be accurate, it is important
    that the observer concentrate on the task at hand
    and direct his primary interest to the purposes of
    the observation. Many a motorist has had the
    experience of losing his way on a trip because he
    was directing his attention elsewhere and missed
    the highway markers. This kind of faulty observation
    is costly not only to travelers; in the school
    situation, it can be costly to the individual being
    observed and damaging to the aims of guidance. If
    pupil analysis is to be based, at least in part, on
    observations, the observer must be alert and attentive
    to ensure the minimizing of erros in judgment.

9. Data from observations should never be interpreted
    in isolation but should be integrated with all other
    information available for pupil analysis.
    Integrating information not only ensures a more
    accurate interpretation but provides the opportunity

to validate the observer's report and to evaluate
in general the observation techniques employed.
(pp. 111-113)

OBSERVATION REPORTS

Observation reports represent an application of the guidelines discussed and serve to increase the effectiveness of
observation for measuring and evaluating pupil progress.
Observations are most frequently reported through rating scales,
check lists, anecdotal records, sociometric techniques and
self-report inventories. These tools and their uses are
described in this section.

Rating Scales

Rating scales are systematic procedures for obtaining
and reporting the judgments of the observer. They usually
present a list of descriptive or qualitative words or phrases
which are checked by the rater and indicate the degree to
which each attribute is present. Blood and Budd (1972)
list three basic types of rating scales: (1) the numerical
rating scale, (2) the graphic scale, and (3) the descriptive
graphic rating scales.

Numerical rating scale. The numerical rating scale is one
of the simplest types of rating scales where the rater checks
or circles a number to indicate the degree to which a trait
or characteristic is present. In most cases the largest
number is high, 1 is low, and the other numbers represent
intermediate values. An example of items adapted from
Gronlund (1971) on a numerical rating scale follows:

Instructions: Indicate the extent to which this pupil
participates in class discussions by
encircling the appropriate number. The
numbers represent the following values:
5 - outstanding, 4 - above average,
3 - average, 2 - below average, and
1 - unsatisfactory

1. To what extent does the pupil
participate in discussions?   1 2 3 4 5

2. To what extent are the comments
related to the topic under
discussion?   1 2 3 4 5

Figure 16 gives another example of a numerical rating scale.

Graphic rating scale. The graphic rating scale differs from the numerical rating scale in two ways. First, it uses words rather than numbers to indicate scales along the scale; second, it employs a line to indicate the continuum for the trait or behavior to be observed with the understanding that the individual may fall at any point along this continuum (Blood and Budd, 1972). An example of two items on a graphic rating scale follows (Gronlund, 1971):

Instructions: Indicate the degree to which this pupil contributes to class discussion by placing an (x) anywhere along the horizontal line under each item.

1. To what extent does the pupil participate in discussion?

```
 ┌────────┬──────────┬──────────┬────────────┐
 never   seldom   occasionally   frequently   always
```

2. To what extent are the comments related to the topic under discussion?

```
 ┌────────┬──────────┬──────────┬────────────┐
 never   seldom   occasionally   frequently   always
```

Figure 17 shows another example of a graphic rating scale.

Descriptive graphic rating scale. The descriptive graphic rating scale is similar to the graphic rating scale, except that instead of using one or two words to indicate the points on a scale, it uses a more elaborate description of the behavior to be observed. The advantage of this approach is that it enables the observer to compare the performance he sees with a description of typical performance at any point along the scale. An example follows (Gronlund, 1971):

Instructions: Make your ratings on each of the following characteristics by placing an (x) anywhere along the horizontal line, under each item. In the space for comments, include anything that helps clarify your rating.

160

Guide For Evaluating Research Papers

Name of student_____ Date_____

Rating scale
5 4 3 2 1

I. Problem   Ratings
      Rating for clearness of statement,
      conciseness, limitation of problem,
      etc.
                                                      _____

II. Method
      A. Rating for statement of method
      B. Rating for research ability   _____
          indicated
                                                      _____

III. The Literature
       Rating for adequacy of the review
       and the command of sources   _____

IV. Treatment and presentation of results
       Rating for research ability indicated   _____

V. Mechanical organization
      A. Features (check presence – one
          point for each)
          1. Preface
          2. Table of contents   _____
          3. List of tables
          4. Bibliography
      B. Rating for organization of tables
      C. Rating for organization of figures   _____
      D. Rating for form of citations and
          bibliography
                                                      _____

VI. English
       Rating for spelling, punctuation,
       diction, etc.
                                                      _____

Score _____

Grade _____

Figure 16. A Numerical Rating Scale. From Don F.
Blood and William C. Budd, _Educational Measurement
and Evaluation_ (New York: Harper & Row Publishers,
1972) p. 52. Reprinted with permission.

Scale for Evaluating Performance on a Brass Instrument
_____

Name_____ Date_____

Directions: Place a check mark at the appropriate place on
each scale to indicate how the student's
performance compares with expected performance
for sixth-grade children.

1. Posture

Below average   Average   Above average

2. Holding of instrument

Below average   Average   Above average

3. Embouchure placement

Below average   Average   Above average

4. Breath control and support

Below average   Average   Above average

5. Fingering

Below average   Average   Above average

6. Instrument care

Below average   Average   Above average
_____

Figure 17. A Graphic Rating Scale. From Don F. Blood
and William C. Budd, Educational Measurement and
Evaluation (New York: Harper & Row Publishers, 1972)
p. 53. Reprinted with permission.

1. To what extent does the pupil participate in discussions?

```
┌──────────────┬──────────────┬──────────────┐
```

never participates;   participates as   participates more
quiet, passive   much as other   than any other
                         group members   group member

Comment:

2. To what extent are the comments related to the topic under discussion?

```
┌──────────────┬──────────────┬──────────────┐
```

comments ramble,   comments usually   comments are
distract from   pertinent, occa-   always related
topic   sionally wanders   to topic
                         from topic

Comment:

Figure 18 gives an example of a descriptive graphic rating scale.

Gibson and Higgins (1966) list 7 uses of the rating scale:

1. Rating scales provide for the evaluation of pupils in areas not covered by their academic records.

    Academic records permit only limited evaluation and understanding of the individual pupil. Rating scales assist in the identification and analysis of a wide variety of other characteristics important to understanding a pupil more fully.

2. Rating scales may indicate patterns of growth and development.

    Where collected and summarized over a period of time, they can contribute to an understanding of pupil growth and development and may indicate behavioral trends.

3. Rating scales provide clues for counseling.

    Rating scales can be specifically designed to alert counselors to pupils who, on the basis of the rater's responses, appear to need counseling. Pupils who receive consistently negative ratings on given items and who reveal certain patterns of ratings may benefit from assistance.

Scale For Evaluating Proposed Room Adjustments in Home Economics

Name _____

I. Function		
1	3	5
Little evidence that the needs of the family were considered.	Evidence of consideration of family needs. Traffic patterns considered.	Excellent evaluation of the needs of family. Traffic patterns are well thought out, as well as window spaces, and other points of emphasis.

II. Color		
1	3	5
Little evidence of thought to color and its dramatic effects.	Color scheme included but there is need to show general areas of color in the room.	An excellent illustration on areas of color; appears to be a livable color scheme – variety in color.

III. Lighting		
1	3	5
Little evidence of thought to useful and decorative purposes of lighting.	A good arrangement of lighting effects, including both general and area lighting.	Creative and functional use of lighting.

IV. Window Treatments		
1	3	5
Little evidence of thought given to window treatment. Color and style not clear.	Ordinary treatment of window space.	Creative window treatment and good illustration of desired effect (type of fabric which would go well in room).

164

Scale for Evaluating Proposed Room Adjustments in Home Economics (Cont'd.)

V. Elements of Design

1	3	5
Little thought to design elements. Room appears unbalanced, has no apparent rhythm and is not to scale.	The room appears balanced. Some application of rhythm principle. Room has some unity.	Excellent balance of room; all parts of the room work together. The rhythm gives unity to the room.

Score _____

Grade _____

Note: The scale in this Figure uses numbers along the top of the line representing the continuum so a score can be derived for the project.

Figure 18. A Descriptive Graphic Rating Scale. From Don F. Blood and William C. Budd, Educational Measurement and Evaluation (New York: Harper & Row Publishers, 1972) p. 55. Reprinted with permission.

4. Rating scales are useful in preparing reports to parents.
   Rating scales can add new dimensions to reports to parents and provide valuable background information for the parent conference.

5. Rating scales are an aid in the preparation of recommendations.
   The school counselor is frequently called on to make recommendations for awards, scholarships, college admissions, or job placement. Use of rating scales enables him to secure the evaluations of others who may know the pupil well and whose firsthand reactions are invaluable in the preparation of such recommendations.

6. Rating scales help pupils see how others see them.
   Rating scales can contribute to a pupil's self-understanding, for they permit him to note his strengths and weaknesses as judged by others. He may draw inferences from variation and consensus in ratings of specific items. Rating scales also enable him to compare his own self-assessment with the assessments given him by others.

7. Rating scales may motivate the pupil.
   Where a student has the opportunity to compare his ratings, he may be motivated to improve them. A knowledge of his weaknesses, as indicated by ratings, may stimulate him to greater efforts. (pp. 122–123)

The improvement of ratings requires careful attention to selection of the characteristics to be rated, design of the rating form, and conditions under which the ratings are obtained. Gronlund (1971) lists 6 principles who summarize the most important considerations in these areas. Since the descriptive graphic rating scale is the most generally useful form for school purposes, the principles are directed specifically toward the construction and use of this type of rating scale.

1. Characteristics should be educationally significant. Rating scales, like other evaluation instruments, must be in harmony with the objectives and desired learning outcomes of the school. Thus, when constructing or selecting a rating scale the best guide for determining what characteristics are most significant is our list of specific learning

outcomes. Where these have been clearly stated in behavioral terms, it is often simply a matter of selecting those that can be most effectively evaluated by ratings and then modifying the statements to fit the rating format.

2. <u>Characteristics</u> <u>should</u> <u>be</u> <u>directly</u> <u>observable</u>. There are two aspects to this. First, the characteristics should be limited to those that occur in school situations so that the teacher has an opportunity to observe them. Second, they should be characteristics that are clearly visible to an observer. Overt behaviors like participation in classroom discussion, clear enunciation, and skill in social relations can be readily observed and reliably rated. However, less tangible types of behavior, such as <u>interest</u> in the opposite sex, <u>feeling</u> of inferiority, and <u>attitude</u> toward minority groups, tend to be unreliably rated because their presence must be inferred from outward signs which are indefinite, variable, and easily faked. Whenever possible, we should confine our ratings to those characteristics which can be observed and judged directly.

3. <u>Characteristics</u> <u>and</u> <u>points</u> <u>on</u> <u>the</u> <u>scale</u> <u>should</u> <u>be</u> <u>clearly</u> <u>defined</u>. Many of the errors in rating arise from the use of general, vague trait characterizations and inadequate identification of the scale points. The brief descriptions used with the descriptive graphic rating scale help overcome this weakness. They not only clarify the meaning of the points on the scale but they also contribute to a fuller understanding of each characteristic being rated. Where it is infeasible or inconvenient to use a descriptive scale, as on the back of a school report card, a separate sheet of instructions can be used to provide the desired behavioral descriptions.

4. <u>Between</u> <u>three</u> <u>and</u> <u>seven</u> <u>rating</u> <u>positions</u> <u>should</u> <u>be</u> <u>provided</u> <u>and</u> <u>raters</u> <u>should</u> <u>be</u> <u>permitted</u> <u>to</u> <u>mark</u> <u>at</u> <u>intermediate</u> <u>points</u>. The exact number of points to be designated on a particular scale is determined largely by the nature of the judgments to be made. In areas permitting only crude judgments, fewer scale positions are needed. There is usually no advantage in going beyond the 7-point scale, however. Only

rarely can we make finer discriminations than this, and we provide for those few situations by allowing the rater to mark between points if he so desires.

5. <u>Raters</u> <u>should</u> <u>be</u> <u>instructed</u> <u>to</u> <u>omit</u> <u>ratings</u> <u>where</u> <u>they</u> <u>feel</u> <u>unqualified</u> <u>to</u> <u>judge</u>. Rating scales to evaluate personal-social adjustment are apt to contain some characteristics which the teacher has had little or no opportunity to observe. To require ratings on such traits merely introduces error into the descriptions of the pupil. It is far better to permit the rater to omit the ratings. Some rating forms provide a place to check "unable to judge" or "insufficient opportunity to observe" for each characteristic. Others provide a space for comments after each characteristic, where it is possible either to justify the rating given or to note the reason for not making a rating.

6. <u>Ratings</u> <u>from</u> <u>several</u> <u>observers</u> <u>should</u> <u>be</u> <u>combined</u>, <u>wherever</u> <u>possible</u>. The pooled ratings of several teachers will generally provide a more reliable description of pupil behavior than that obtained from any one teacher. In averaging ratings, the personal biases of individual raters tend to cancel each other out. Combined ratings are especially applicable at the high school level, where specific teacher-pupil contact is limited but each pupil has classes with a number of teachers. They are less feasible at the elementary school level, since here we are apt to have only the ratings of the pupil's one regular teacher. The lack of additional raters at this level, however, is at least partially offset by the greater opportunity for the teacher to observe his pupils in a variety of situations. Furthermore, the smaller number of elementary teachers in a school makes it easier to detect and allow for common biases, such as the tendency to overrate or underrate pupils. (pp. 427-428)

Check Lists

Check lists are instruments that consist of a list of personality traits or characteristics that the observer indicates as being present or absent. This type of instrument is easy to administer and simple to complete. However, it does not provide the degree to which a pupil possesses a given characteristic. Figures 19 and 20 are examples of common forms of observation check lists.

OBSERVATION CHECKLIST

Personal characteristics of _____
                                    (name of student)

Observed by (name or code) _____

Periods (dates of observation: from _____ to _____

Conditions under which student was observed: _____

Instructions: Place a check mark in the blanks to the left of any of the
following traits you believe to characteristic of the student.

POSITIVE TRAITS

___ 1. Neat in appearance
___ 2. Enjoys good health
___ 3. Regular in attendance
___ 4. Courteous
___ 5. Concerned for others
___ 6. Popular with other students
___ 7. Displays leadership ability
___ 8. Has a good sense of humor
___ 9. Shows initiative
___ 10. Industrious
___ 11. Has a pleasant disposition
___ 12. Mature
___ 13. Respects property of others

NEGATIVE TRAITS

___ 16. Unreliable
___ 17. Uncooperative
___ 18. Domineering
___ 19. Self-centered
___ 20. Rude
___ 21. Sarcastic
___ 22. Boastful
___ 23. Dishonest
___ 24. Resents authority
___ 25. A bully
___ 26. Overly aggressive
___ 27. Shy and withdrawn
___ 28. Cries easily

OBSERVATION CHECKLIST (Cont'd.)

14. Nearly always does his best
15. Adjusts easily to different situations

29. Deceitful
30. Oversolicitous

Comments: _____

_____

_____

_____

_____

Figure 19. Observation Checklist. From TECHNIQUES OF GUIDANCE: AN APPROACH TO PUPIL ANALYSIS by Robert L. Gibson. Copyright 1966, Science Research Associates, Inc. Reproduced by permission of the publisher.

Concern for Others

Note: Check each child two or three times during the term to determine if growth has taken place.

School _____

Date _____

Behavior to be observed	Names of Children							
Is sensitive to needs and problems of others								
Helps others meet needs and solve problems								
Willingly shares ideas and materials								
Accepts suggestions and help								
Makes constructive suggestions								
Sticks to group plans and decisions								
Works courteously and happily with others								
Gives encouragement to others								
Respects the property of others								
Enjoys group work								
Thanks others for help								
Commends others for contributions								

Figure 20. Checklist for Evaluating Pupil's "Concern for Others." From John U. Michaelis, Social Studies for Children in a Democracy (Englewood Cliffs, New Jersey: Prentice-Hall Inc., 1963). Reprinted with permission.

Anecdotal Records

Anecdotal records consist of objective descriptions of pupil behavior in a particular environmental setting, an interpretation of the behavior by the observer writing the description, and a recommendation for future action based on the incident and its interpretation (Froehlich and Hoyt, 1959, p. 235).

A good anecdote is one that has been recorded. Lien (1971) lists the uses, characteristics and contents of anecdotes:

1. When anecdotal records are used
   a. Observation of growth toward understandings, skills, and attitudes
   b. Diagnosis of academic and social problems
   c. Social development and skills
   d. Health and physical growth
   e. Provide feeder data for rating scales, check-lists, and cumulative record

2. Characteristics of an anecdote
   a. It is factual: it records only the actual event, incident, uncolored by the feelings, inter-pretations, or biases of the observer.
   b. It is an observation of only one incident.
   c. It is an observation of an incident which is considered important and significant in the growth and/or development of the pupil.
   d. It is short and informal, yet gives pertinent information.
   e. It contains information which may be either complimentary or uncomplimentary.
   f. It shows growth or lack of growth toward certain objectives or purposes for which the teacher is teaching and for which the pupils are striving.
   g. It serves its best purposes when a periodic summary is made of individual anecdotes over a period of time to reveal consistent patterns of growth or regression.

3. What it contains
   a. Identity of the pupil observed: name and class or activity
   b. Date of observation
   c. Name of observer
   d. Incident

Optional
(1) Interpretation of behavior
(2) Suggestions or recommendations concerning
growth and behavior   (p. 144)

Anecdotal records, like any other instrument or tool,
have limitations. The limitations of the anecdotal record
have been listed by Traxler (1949).

1. It is apparent, of course, that an anecdotal record
can be valuable only if the original observation is
accurate and is correctly recorded; otherwise, it
may be worse than useless.

2. Many persons find it extremely difficult to write
with complete objectivity, but practice will do a
great deal to overcome the tendency to intersperse
the report of behavior with statements of opinion.

3. A pernicious but fortunately rare use of anecdotal
records is the employment of them for defense
purposes.

4. It is evident that there is danger in lifing a behavior incident out of the social setting in which
it occurred and reporting it in isolation.

5. At best, only a small proportion of the total
number of significant behavior incidents for any
pupil will find their way into anecdotal records.

6. Some persons fear that anecdotes, through preserving
a record of unfortunate behavior incidents on the
part of certain pupils, may prejudice their success
long afterward, when the behavior is no longer
typical of them.

7. It cannot be too strongly emphasized that the
adoption of a system of anecdotal records is no
small commitment and that it will inevitably add
to the load of the entire staff, particularly the
counselors and the clerical staff.

8. There is some danger that anecdotal records will
throw the need for better adjustment of certain
pupils into such high relief that too marked an
effort will be made to short-cut the adjustment
process.

173

9. Undesirable behavior because of its nuisance aspect,
    is likely to make a stronger impression on teachers
    than desirable behavior.

10. Occasionally teachers will observe incidents that
    are not all typical of the behavior of the pupil
    concerned. (pp. 17-20)

SOCIOMETRIC TECHNIQUES

Sociometry or the sociometric technique has to do with
studying how the student's classmates see him and with his
degree of social acceptance by them. It is based on pupils'
choices of companions for some group situation or activity.
Questions are devised by the teacher which will encourage
pupils to reveal their true feelings about other members of
the class. Adams (1964) suggests the following types of
questions:

1. Whom do you wish to sit next to in the classroom?

2. With whom would you like to work on a committee?

3. Whom would you like as a companion on a class project?

4. Who are your best friends?

5. With whom do you like to associate after school?
    (pp. 281-286)

Gronlund (1959) describes the sociometric process in
great detail. The tabulation and organization of sociometric results are of particular interest at this point.
Prior to discussing these facets of sociometry, however, it
is necessary to explain pertinent terms used in this process.
Gronlund uses these terms:

1. Sociometric Question or Sociometric Criterion:
    Provides the basis of the choice which the student
    must make.

2. Sociometric Status, Social Status, or Group Status:
    Refers to the number of choices each individual
    receives from the other members of the group. In
    other words, it is the number of times an individual
    is chosen by other students on the basis of the
    sociometric question.

174

3. <u>Sociometric</u> <u>Structure</u>, <u>Social</u> <u>Structure</u>, <u>or</u> <u>Group</u>
   <u>Structure</u>: Refers to the pattern of choices to and
   from individuals, revealing the network of inter-
   personal relations among group members.

4. <u>Sociogram</u>: The term applied to the diagram which
   shows visually this sociometric structure.

5. <u>Sociometric</u> <u>Test</u>: The method used to evaluate group
   structure.

6. <u>Star</u>: An individual who receives a large number of
   choices on a sociometric test. The number of choices
   received in order to be designated a star varies with
   the number of choices permitted in the sociometric
   test and the number of pupils taking the test.

7. <u>Isolate</u>: A physical member of the group who is
   psychologically isolated from the other group members.
   He receives no choice on the test. Outsider or social
   island are other designations for the isolate.

8. <u>Neglectee</u>: The individual who receives relatively
   few choices on the sociometric test. Negative choices
   result when the sociometric question requests students
   to indicate those whom they least prefer for a
   specified activity.

9. <u>Rejectee</u>: The individual who receives negative
   choices on a sociometric test. Rejected choices
   result when the sociometric questions requests
   students to indicate those whom they do not prefer
   for a specified activity.

10. <u>Mutual</u> <u>Choice</u>, <u>Reciprocated</u> <u>Choice</u>, <u>or</u> <u>Pair</u>: Two
    individuals who have chosen each other on the same
    sociometric criterion.

11. <u>Sociometric</u> <u>Clique</u>: A situation in which a number
    of individuals choose each other on the same socio-
    metric criterion, but give relatively few choices
    to individuals outside their group.

12. <u>Sociometric</u> <u>Cleavage</u>: The lack of sociometric
    choices between two or more subgroups. (pp. 3-6)

The sociometric technique is a relatively easy technique
based on pupils' choices of other pupils for a group situation

or activity. Gronlund (1959) suggests a typical sociometric form which is shown in Figure 21.

The pupil's sociometric choices should be organized in some systematic fashion, if the classroom teacher is to interpret and use them properly. A complete record of the sociometric results can be obtained by tabulating the choices in a matrix table as suggested by Gronlund (1959) and reproduced in Figure 22.

A perusal of Figure 22 suggests the following (Gronlund, 1971):

1. The pupils' names are listed down the side of the table and are numbered from 1 to 20.

2. These same numbers, corresponding to the pupils' names, are then placed across the top of the table so that each pupil's choices can be recorded in the appropriate column.

3. The X's represent rejection choices, while the circled numbers indicate mutual choices. Mutual choices are always an equal number of cells from the diagonal line, in each corresponding column and row.

4. The number of choices a pupil receives is used as an indication of his social acceptance by peers:
   a. Stars - Pupils receiving nine or more choices.
   b. Isolates - Pupils receiving no choices.
   c. Neglectees - Those receiving one choice.
   d. Remaining Pupils - Those who fail somewhere above or below average; are given no special name.
   e. Rejectees - Pupils receiving only rejection choices.
   f. Mutual Choices - Where pupils choose each other. (pp. 442-444)

While the matrix table is used in organizing sociometric data for determining the social acceptance of individual pupils, the sociogram is used to depict a picture of the social structure of the group. Gronlund (1959) suggests a typical sociogram which is reproduced in Figure 23 and is based in the previous Figure.

A perusal of Figure 23 indicates that (Gronlund, 1971):

1. Concentric circles form the sociogram on which to plot the data.

176

Name_____ Date_____

During the next few weeks we will be changing our seats around, working in small groups and playing some group games. Now that we all know each other by name, you can help me arrange groups that work and play best together. You can do this by writing the names of the children you would like to have sit near you, to have work with you, and to have play with you. You may choose anyone in this room you wish, including those pupils who are absent. Your choices will not be seen by anyone else. Give first name and initial of last name.

Make your choices carefully so the groups will be the way you really want them. I will try to arrange the groups so that each pupil gets at least two of his choices. Sometimes it is hard to give everyone his first few choices so be sure to make five choices for each question.

Remember!
1. Your choices must be from pupils in this room, including those who are absent.

2. You should give the first name and the initial of the last name.

3. You should make all five choices for each question.

4. You may choose a pupil for more than one group if you wish.

5. Your choices will not be seen by anyone else.

I would choose to sit near these children:

1. _____   3. _____
2. _____   4. _____
            5. _____

I would choose to work with these children:

1. _____   3. _____
2. _____   4. _____
            5. _____

I would choose to play with these children:

1. _____   3. _____
2. _____   4. _____
            5. _____

Figure 21. A Sociometric Form. From N. E. Gronlund, Sociometry in the Classroom (New York: Harper & Row, 1959). Reprinted with permission.

Figure 22. A Matrix of Sociometric Choices. From N. E. Gronlund, Sociometry in the Classroom (New York: Harper & Row Publishers, 1959). Reproduced with permission.

Note: SS = Same Sex   OS = Opposite Sex   X = Rejection

Name	Choices Given SS	Choices Given OS	Rejections Given SS
1 John A.	4	1	2
2 Mike A.	5	0	2
3 Jim B.	5	0	0
4 Henry D.	4	1	0
5 Bob F.	4	1	0
6 Bill H.	2	3	0
7 George L.	5	0	2
8 Dick N.	4	1	0
9 Dale P.	5	0	1
10 Pete V.	4	1	0
11 Mary A.	3	2	0
12 Betty A.	5	0	0
13 Karen B.	4	1	1
14 Lois C.	4	1	0
15 Sharon J.	5	0	0
16 Ann K.	3	2	0
17 Mary M.	4	1	0
18 Sue R.	4	0	0
19 Pat S.	5	0	0
20 Carol W.	4	1	1

Central (School)
5A (Class)
F. R. Young (Teacher)

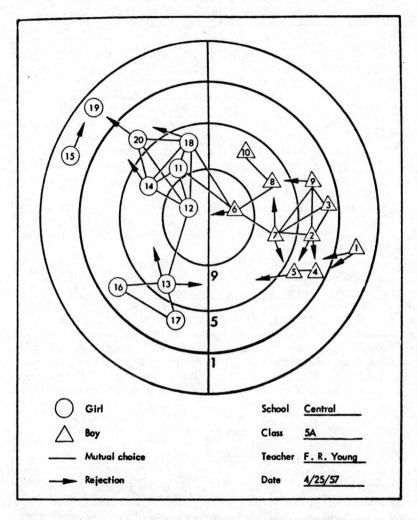

Figure 23. A Sociogram. From N. E. Gronlund,
Sociometry in the Classroom (New York: Harper &
Row Publishers, 1959). Reproduced with permission.

2. Pupils in the <u>star</u> category are placed in the center
   of the target; isolates are placed in the other ring;
   the remaining pupils are placed between these extremes in terms of the number of choices received.

3. Boys are represented by triangles, while the girls are
   represented by circles.

4. The sociogram illustrates the common social con-
   figurations that can be expected in most group
   structures. Girls number 12, 11, 14, 18, and 20
   form a very cohesive <u>clique</u>. Girls number 13, 16,
   and 17 form a <u>triangle</u>. Boys number 10, 8, and 6
   form a <u>chain</u> of mutual choices and boys number 4 and 5
   form a mutual <u>pair</u>. There seems to be a social
   <u>cleavage</u> between boys and girls except for a few
   mutual cross-sex choices of boy number 6. Pupils
   1, 15, and 19 are <u>isolated</u> from the group, while
   pupil number 19 is actively <u>rejected</u> by four girls.
   (pp. 444-446)

Although sociograms portray social relations in a
classroom for <u>a particular situation</u>, they do not indicate
<u>why</u> a specific social structure evolved nor <u>what</u> should be
done about it. It is, therefore, necessary to supplement
sociometric techniques with other sources such as observations, tests, etc. Another caution in the use of
sociometric techniques is that the social structure of a
class <u>may</u> change from one situation to another. They may,
therefore, be unreliable from one situation to another
depending on the type of project to be engaged in. They are,
nevertheless, useful as another source of information in
measuring and evaluating pupil progress.

CUMULATIVE RECORDS AND CASE STUDIES

Theoretically and ideally <u>cumulative records</u> present an
organized, progressive record of information about the individual pupil which distinguishes him from all other students.
They represent a storehouse for data about a pupil, yielding
a maximum of data in a minimum of space.

Case studies represent a commonly used method of
summarizing data about an individual and are the most comprehensive of evaluation techniques. They seek to present a
cumulative picture of the total individual by giving a
full-length study of a pupil that shows his development and
the interrelations of the factors governing his current status.

180

The information employed in their use is gathered from all available reliable resources. They contain interpretations, recommendations for action, and provisions for followup.

DeBlassie (1971) describes the cumulative record and the case study and then proceeds to show how a well developed cumulative record represents a case study in miniature. The article is reproduced in its entirity.

Commentary:

RICHARD R. DE BLASSIE/New Mexico State University

THE ELEMENTARY SCHOOL CUMULATIVE RECORD: A CASE STUDY IN MINIATURE

Historically the role of the elementary school has been the development of the basic skills (i.e., the 3 R's) in pupils. In the last few decades, however, the educational goals of the elementary school have been expanded to include the development of affective as well as cognitive skills. More specifically, education as an institution in our society has been charged with the responsibility of developing the "well-rounded" individual, academically, psychologically, socially, etc. Education has made great strides in meeting this charge particularly in regard to a genuine concern for the individual which currently undergirds the American educational enterprise. The burden for helping every individual pupil develop his potentialities, while at the same time recognizing him as a unique entity endowed with individual differences, would seem to fall on the shoulders of the classroom teacher. Wrenn (1962) notes that this goal is what makes the American classroom teacher's task the most difficult in the world.

There is a consensus among educators that to fulfill these expectations, teachers need the assistance of the guidance specialist, and that guidance services are an integral part of the total educational program. As a result, guidance programs are being developed extensively in elementary schools. These programs are evolving from only crisis-oriented activities to full partnership, developmental functions in the school systems. These services constitute a full third dimension to the two historic divisions of the school: instruction and administration.

Two guidance techniques that are frequently used by counselors and teachers in the elementary school to complement the classroom teacher's effort to aid the individual child to develop maximally are the cumulative record and the case study. The purpose of this paper is to provide elementary school teachers with an indication of how the cumulative record can serve as a "ready-made" case study through which she can synthesize data about an individual

NATIONAL CATHOLIC GUIDANCE CONFERENCE JOURNAL, Winter, 1971, Vol. 15, No. 2.
Reprinted with permission.

as she attempts to help him develop academically, psychologically, and socially.

The Case Study

A case study is herein defined as: A systematic, continuous, differential, and personalized study and interpretation of the individual pupil, his environment, and his experiences as they relate to his development and growth. The case study procedure results in (1) an accumulation of information; (2) some hypotheses suggested by the assembled information; and (3) a further search for data to validate the hypotheses. Case studies are designed to enable the reader to understand a pupil well enough so that effective planning can be done for the next steps in his development. They are also designed to encourage a rather complete and longitudinal study of the individual by the use of many techniques and to synthesize the many parts into a valid dynamic picture of him as a whole.

Suggested case study guides and outlines can be found in several sources. One example comes from the Department of Education of the State of Ohio (1965).

Outline for Use in a Case Study

I. Preliminary statement

—Statement of the situation leading to the study for the maximum development of a boy or girl.

—When a problem is involved, statement of the apparent problem, its probable immediate cause, and other circumstances surrounding the case.

II. Summary of available data (from records, visits counselor's record, etc.)

A. Present status (Age, Sex, Grade-class-teacher's name)

B. Physical Status (Physical appearance and history—general impression made by the child; obvious physical limitations; mannerisms, neatness, clothing; illnesses—general conditions); Medical examination results.

C. Educational status (Present school achievement; promotions—retardations and causes; relation with individual teachers; tests or other measures of achievement or aptitude; other relevant information from counselors and teachers.)

D. Personal—social traits (Personality—general tone; Attitude toward home, friends, self, family; Hobbies, play life, leisure time activities; Educational and vocational ambitions; Marked likes and dislikes, fear; any special or social problems.)

E. Home and family (Individuals at home; apparent economic level—cultural resources; relation with the home; record at social agencies; home cooperation).

F. Activities or work experience (Part-time or summer; employer's reaction; occupational plans and goals).

III. Interview with student

A. Assess attitudes (Toward school, home, self and others).

B. Explore student's perception of precipitating factors if a complaint exists.

C. Collection of other relevant data

IV. Analysis of data

V. Recommendations for and plan for accenting optimal development or in the case of treatment, therapy, or remediation (Immediate desired outcomes; Long range desired outcomes).

VI. Follow-up to determine progress and to adjust recommendations

A. Reports (Teachers, others)

B. Observations (Interview with subject; Informal throughout school by teachers, counselors).

VII. Summary

If one closely examines the outline given above he will be struck with the fact that the form, or outline, of the case study is an important aid to keeping the information well organized and for insuring completeness of the case report. But, it is also clear that the case outline is only a guide; it does not gather information, nor collate and synthesize it, nor test its validity, nor interpret its meaning. However, the real merit of the outline lies in its close resemblance to data usually recorded in the standard cumulative record.

The Cumulative Record

The cumulative record is designed as a vehicle for accumulating information about a pupil in the course of his progress through school and combines many records in one and is a comprehensive accumulation of the varied kinds of information essential to individual pupil development, guidance, and accounting. While cumulative records vary from school system to school system, most cumulative records have a space for the following information:

1. Basic personal data
2. Home background
3. School background
4. Academic record
5. Attendance record
6. Health and Physical development
7. Guidance test results-scholastic aptitude, achievement, etc.
8. Educational-vocational interests and plans
9. Work and other significant out-of-school experiences
10. School activities
11. Personality characteristics
12. Special comments, interpretations, summarizations, and follow-up statements

The Central Thesis

One of the major limitations of the case study, according to some, is the amount of time consumed in assembling data for the study. The central thesis of this paper is

that this a ludicrous rationalization. Since one of the first tasks in making a case study is to get the facts about the individual the initial stages of the study are highly similar to the data recorded in the cumulative record. Thus, if the school has a systematic and well-maintained cumulative-record system, gathering data for case studies is accomplished as a matter of routine; and by means of information-retrieval methods the data may be made available immediately. The cumulative record, then, represents in effect the case history on the individual. Once the data in the cumulative record are synthesized, analyzed, and interpreted, and hypotheses about an individual drawn therefrom they become a case study. The cumulative record then, it would seem, should be regarded as a *case-study in miniature*.

Implications

Although much has been written about case studies and cumulative records, one is awed by the lack of information dealing with relating and integrating the two techniques for studying the individual and helping him to develop and progress to his maximum potential. It seems as though the case study can logically flow from a well-maintained cumulative record system. It would seem that elementary school administrators should encourage classroom teachers to contribute to the cumulative records in some logical, systematic fashion in order to insure a longitudinal, development record which would ultimately serve as a basis for studying the individual and aiding him in becoming a "well-rounded" individual. If teachers are found lacking in these skills, it would behoove administrators to establish in-service programs to help these teachers develop them. In-service programs could also focus on helping teachers develop skills in analyzing and interpreting such data.

An additional suggestion is made by this writer. Perhaps a committee consisting of the elementary principal, the counselor, and some teachers could be formulated for the purpose of designing a cumulative record which would more closely follow the format of the case study outline suggested above (or a similar one). Such a cumulative record would indeed become an ongoing case study and would eliminate the notion that "it is impossible to do case study on every individual student."

In summary, the cumulative record represents a potential case study in miniature. If education is to continue verbalizing its concern for the individual student, what better way to prove this concern than by providing such a systematic procedure for insuring that the individual does not become an obscure generalization based on averages computed from groups.

REFERENCES

Enclosure with January-February, 1965 issue of *Ohio News and Views.* Columbus, Ohio: State Department of Education, Division of Guidance and Testing.

Gibson, Robert L.; and Higgins, Robert. *Techniques of guidance: an approach to pupil analysis.* Chicago: Science Research Associates, 1966.

Saltzman, Glenn A. and Peters, Herman J. *Pupil personnel services: selected readings.* Itasca, Illinois: F. E. Peacock, 1967.

Wrenn, C. Gilbert. *The counselor in a changing world.* Washington, D. C.: American Personnel Guidance Association, 1962.

Chapter IX

EVALUATION: GRADING, MARKING, AND INTERPRETING

Previous chapters have defined and discussed the term <u>evaluation</u> as the interpretation of data or measurements which are collected about pupils. This chapter focuses on ways that the classroom teacher can interpret and assign meaning to various data that he has collected in attempting to make evaluative judgments about the progress of his pupils in the classroom. The emphasis will be: assigning grades, the use of test results, and reporting pupil progress.

Prior to discussing grading, the use of test results, and reporting, however, it may be worthwhile to consider some goals to strive for in improving evaluation. Biehler (1974) lists the following goals to strive for in improving evaluation:

1. Do everything possible to arrange evaluation experiences so that they lead to feelings of success.

2. Minimize public comparisons and competition among students.

3. Be aware that learning ability is not the same in all pupils, but use this knowledge as the basis for a value-added approach to education; that is, give extra assistance to those who need it.

4. Do everything possible to make evaluations fair and objective - guard against the halo effect, cognitive dissonance, projection, and the impact of unconscious likes and dislikes.

5. Make the most of the characteristics of tests; provide a standard situation, obtain records of performance in permanent form, compare student performance to a fixed set of criteria.

6. Try to use tests so that they emphasize reinforcement of correct responses and not punish wrong responses.

7. Arrange evaluation so that it identifies omissions and weaknesses that need to be corrected before the student moves on to more advanced material.

8. Try to use evaluation as a motivating device by en-
   couraging students to set and achieve respectable
   (and realistic) goals.

9. Stress the importance of establishing and meeting
   standards. As much as possible, use tests to promote
   self-competition and improvement.

10. Set up exams so that they provide feedback for you to
    use in improving instruction.

11. When appropriate, state specific instructional ob-
    jectives, determine if they have been reached, and
    take steps to supply remedial instruction.

12. Do everything possible to reduce pressure and tension.

13. Try to make tests functional in the sense that students
    recognize or are made aware that the information
    requested is being learned for good reasons. (p. 524)

GRADING

Every classroom teacher is faced with the reality of, at
some point, transforming or converting scores into grades
which are intended to accomplish three broad purposes:

1. Communication to Students and Parents. Marks provide
   useful and efficient data which can be used to
   communicate with students and their parents. Marking
   and reporting are essentially information processing
   activities, and might be likened to a communications
   network. Marks are merely the means by which a
   teacher communicates his evaluations about the progress that each student has made toward a specified
   set of educational goals.
        Students have a right and need to learn of their
   progress. In addition to the methods of reporting
   achievement data via rank in class, grade equivalents,
   standard scores, percentile ranks, students seem to
   desire a more "subjective" evaluation of their
   performances. They wish to know if their work is
   outstanding, good, acceptable, or unacceptable. The
   teacher is probably in a better position than anyone
   else to integrate the many factors relating to
   learning and achievement, and communicate his summary to the student.
        Parents, too, have a right and need to learn of the
   educational progress of their progeny. Marks provide

reasonable summarizing appraisals which a parent will find useful in counseling a student about his school work and future educational and vocational plans.

2. <u>Communicating to Present and Future School Personnel</u>. Just as the results of standardized achievement tests can be used to evaluate the overall progress of a particular instructional program and school, so can distributions of marks be used to indicate trend of progress. Such data are useful in making promotional, graduation, transfer, and future educational decisions.

We consider indices of past achievement probably the best single indication of future achievement. College admissions personnel, therefore, view marks as generally indicative of the level of performance to be reached by individual students if admitted to their institution. Marks serve as academic currency useful in the college market place, although their exchange and conversion properties are limited.

Promotional decisions should of course never be made on the basis of marks alone.

3. <u>Motivating Student Learning</u>. In research literature there exists evidence that marks may function to reinforce or inhibit learning. Marks constitute an obvious extrinsic source of motivation. And although we would ideally like learning to result from intrinsic motivation, the gross extrinsic force represented by marks must be reckoned with.

In viewing the motivation function of marks, the importance of defining on what basis the marks are assigned comes into play. If a mark is given only to indicate status at a particular point in time, then it is doubtful if most students will feel challenged to work for higher marks. If, however, marks reflect improvement or achievement relative to ability, students may be spurred to greater efforts. (Payne, 1968, pp. 182-184)

Remmers, et al. (1960) suggest that marking and grading systems should provide the basis for:

1. Information for parents on pupil status or progress.

2. Promotion and graduation.

3. Motivation of school work.

4. Guidance of learning.

5. Guidance of educational and vocational planning.

6. Guidance of personal development.

7. Honors

8. Participation in many school activities.

9. Reports and recommendations to future employers.

10. Data for curriculum studies.

11. Reports to a school which the pupil may attend later.

Problems of Grading

There are a number of problems related to assigning grades and marks. Green (1970) lists seven major problems associated with grading:

1. There is widespread misunderstanding of the meaning of the term "scoring," "grading," and "marking."

2. Course marks often fail to reflect the real course achievement of pupils.

3. Course marks are often based on insufficient evidence of pupil achievement.

4. Many teachers lack clearly defined criteria for assigning course marks or assign them carelessly without serious effort to assess achievement.

5. Teachers often permit such extraneous factors as the halo effect, personality conflicts, class attendance, and discipline to influence pupils' course marks.

6. Teachers, parents, and pupils rarely share an understanding of the nature and extent of achievement represented by specific course marks.

7. Pupils frequently work for a specific course mark rather than to learn as much as possible in a course. (p. 308)

Characteristics of A Good Grading System

Hedges (1969) enumerates twenty-one characteristics of an adequate grading system for the elementary school level, which relate to the junior and senior high school levels as well. He suggests that an adequate grading system:

1. Provides a great deal of information to the parents.

2. Provides information helpful in planning the student's program.

3. Provides information that can be recorded.

4. Accumulates information concerning the methods of teaching and systems of learning which are most effective for particular students.

5. Reveals growth of the student.

6. Goes beyond the record of academic achievement.

7. Eliminates the concept of failure.

8. Reflects student effort.

9. Reduces the opportunity for gross comparisons.

10. Helps the student grow in the ability to evaluate himself.

11. Builds the student's self-image.

12. Provides a basis for student-teacher dialogue.

13. Encourages confidence.

14. Facilitates the student's learning.

15. Is highly specific.

16. Encourages the growth of intrinsic motivation.

17. Recognizes all the objectives of the school.

18. Provides feedback to the school for curriculum revision.

19. Affects the student's study habits positively.

20. Allows for variable pacing of students.

21. Is realistic. (pp. 158-170)

Assigning Letter Grades To Scores

There are a number of ways used to determine grade assignments. There are statistical and nonstatistical methods of assigning grades. Two statistical methods (the <u>standard deviation</u> method and the <u>Q method</u>) and three nonstatistical methods (the <u>per cent method</u>, the <u>natural grouping method</u>, and the <u>Douglas method</u>) will be explained.

Before discussing each of the methods, however, let us recall the 30 raw scores on the Biology Test which were discussed in Chapter III. These scores will formulate the basis for a discussion of the various methods for grading.

98	84	77	71	68	60
94	83	76	70	66	57
93	82	74	70	65	55
89	81	74	70	64	53
88	79	72	69	61	50

The descriptive statistics for the 30 raw scores were as follows:

$(\bar{X})$—Mean = 73
(Mdn)—Median = 72.35 or 72
(Mo)—Mode = 72
(R)—Range = 48
(SD)—Standard Deviation = 11
(Q)—Quartile Deviation = 8.13 or 8

Statistical Methods

1. Standard Deviation Method (M=73; SD=11)

Grade	Determination	Breaks	Points	Grades
A	$M + 1.5\sigma$	73 + 16	89 +	A (4)
B	$M + .5\sigma$ to 1.5σ	73 + 5	78 – 88	B (6)
C	$M \pm .5\sigma$	73 – 5	68 – 77	C (11)
D	$M - 1.5\sigma$	73 – 16	57 – 67	D (6)
F	$M - 1.5\sigma$		56 –	F (3)

30

2. The Q Method (Mdn=72; Q=8)

Grade	Determination	Breaks	Points	Grades
A	Mdn + 2Q	72 + 16	88 +	A (5)
B	Mdn + 1Q	72 + 8	80 – 87	B (4)

C	Mdn – 1Q	72 – 8	64 – 79	C (15)
D	Mdn – 2Q	72 – 16	56 – 63	D (3)
F			55 –	F (3)
				30

Nonstatistical Methods

1. Percentage Method. In this method, a predetermined
    per cent of the possible score for a test is set up
    for each grade. These per cents are usually set as
    a matter of school-wide policy. One such scheme
    follows:

Grade	Breaks	Grades
A	96% – Up	A (1)
B	86% – 95%	B (4)
C	75% – 85%	C (7)
D	70% – 74%	D (7)
F	69% – Less	F (11)
		30

2. Gaps Method. In this method, the division between
    grades is determined by where gaps occur between the
    test scores. Such gaps occur as a result of pure
    chance.

Grade	Breaks	Grades
A	93 – Up	A (3)
B	79 – 92	B (7)
C	66 – 78	C (12)
D	60 – 65	D (4)
F	50–57	F (4)
		30

3. The Douglas Method. This method is named after
    Douglas (1967). It is designed so that no statistical
    measures are used except the range. The method of
    calculation is shown in Figure 24.

    The following chart shows a comparison of the number of
grades assigned in each of the five-letter-grade divisions by
the five methods described above when the same test scores
are used:

Score	f		Steps to be followed in determining letter grades
98	1		1. Begin with the highest score made and number downward consecutively, stopping with the lowest score made. Establish an f column and insert the frequencies.
99			
96			
95		A_4	
94	1		2. Find the range by subtracting the lowest score made from the highest score made plus one (98 + 1 − 50 = 49).
93	1		
92			
91			3. Divide the highest score made into the lowest
89	1		score made to determine how many letter
88	1		grades should be given according to this
87			table:
86			
85		B_5	
84	1		
83	1		
82	1		
81	1		
80			
79	1		4. Divide the number of grades to be given,
78			plus one, into the range to determine the
77	1		number of possible scores to be placed in
76	1		each grade division. Applying these steps
75			we have:
74	2	C_{17}	50 (lowest score) divided by 98 (highest
73			score) gives .51, which indicates that
72	1		four letter grades should be given (Step 3).
71	1		
70	3		49 (the range, Step 2) divided by 5 (the
69	1		number of grades to be given plus 1, (Step
68	1		4) gives with a remainder of 4. This means
67			that 9 possible scores will be placed in
66	1		each grade division except the C group (or
65	1		middle group), where twice the number plus
64	1		any remainder (four in this case) will be
63			placed.
62			5. Begin at the top and count down the number
61	1		of possible scores as determined in Step 4.
60	1		
59			Application:
58			a. Beginning at the top, count down 9
57	1		scores and draw a line between 88 and
56			89 (division between A's and B's).
55	1		b. Count down 9 more scores and draw a
54		D_4	line between 79 and 80 (division between B's and C's).

Fraction Obtained — No. of Grades to be given

Fraction Obtained	No. of Grades to be given
.95 – Up	1
.90 – .94	2
.70 – .89	3
.50 – .69	4
.49 – Less	5

Score	f	Steps to be followed in determining letter grades
53	1	c. Count down 22 more scores (twice the number, 9, for other grades plus the remainder, 4) and draw a line between 57 and 58 (division between C's and D's).
52		
51		
50	1	
N=30		

        d. Count down 9 more scores and draw a line between 49 and 48 (division between D's and F's) which in reality do not exist.

6. Label the sections by grade designation. Place the number of cases (frequencies) in each grade nearby and circle.

7. Note, in Step 3. When less than five letter grades are indicated, the teacher must decide which grades are to be given; that is, whether A's should be given or not.

8. Note, in Step 4. Double the number of possible scores is placed in one division (the middle, if uneven) to obtain a proper "spread" for the average, or middle division.

Figure 24. The Douglas Method for Assigning Letter Grades. From L. M. Douglas, The Secondary Teacher at Work (Boston: D. C. Heath & Co., 1967). Used with permission.

Letter Grade	SD	Q	%-age	Gaps	Douglas
A	4	5	1	3	4
B	6	4	4	7	5
C	11	15	15	12	17
D	6	3	7	4	4
F	3	3	11	4	0

From the above, it should be noted that minor differences exist among the several methods. One may, however, make the decision as to which method is best for a particular situation on the basis of the following criteria (Douglas, 1967):

1. Is the method objective? Would the same grade be assigned if the process were repeated?

2. Is the process relatively simple to compute?

3. Does the method provide for variations in teaching efficiency?

4. Does the method provide allowance for variations in testing efficiency?

5. Does the method make provisions for homogeneous grouping?

To this list, this author would add the following:

1. If the SD or Q methods are used, can it be assumed that the test scores are normally distributed?

2. Does the method assume a heterogeneous group of students?

3. Does the method assume that the test given is one that is valid and reliable and discriminates well between higher scoring and lower scoring pupils?

4. Does the method provide the greatest reward and reinforcement for the largest number of pupils?

USES OF TEST RESULTS

There are a number of uses for which tests can be used in measuring and evaluating pupil progress. Noll and Scannell (1972, pp. 514-554) suggest eleven major purposes for which tests and other measuring instruments are used in schools today. These purposes are listed and briefly described below.

1. <u>Placement</u> <u>and</u> <u>promotion</u>. One of the primary uses of test results of pupils at particular grade levels, promoting, accelerating, or holding them as may be judged appropriate. Ideally, pupils should be placed at levels where they can learn without being unduly discouraged, overworked, or bored. The most useful tool for classification or grade placement is probably a general, standardized school achievement battery. This type of test is also useful for determining the level of a student's achievement when a pupil transfers from one school to another. General intelligence tests are also useful in classifying students, in addition to achievement tests, so that both educational and general development can be taken into account in placing the pupil. In cases involving retention or promotion, the same types of information about the individual will be useful.

2. <u>Homogeneous</u> <u>grouping</u>. Various methods of grouping pupils according to ability are widely practiced, particularly in the elementary grades. The grouping may be done informally and more or less subjectively, as when a teacher of second grade forms her thirty pupils into reading groups of ten to fifteen on the basis of reading ability. Or it may be done formally, as when a hundred pupils in the fifth grade are divided into three classes according to general mental ability.

3. <u>Diagnosis</u> <u>and</u> <u>remedial</u> <u>work</u>. The employment of tests for diagnosis is an instructional function rather than an administrative one. The purpose of a diagnostic test is to find the specific weaknesses and strengths of a pupil in a particular area of study or subject matter. Many achievement tests may be used for diagnosis, but much time and energy are saved and a more systematic analysis is possible when a test is built with diagnosis in mind, if that is to be its function. It is possible, nevertheless, for a teacher to make diagnoses by studying results of standardized achievement tests. By tabulating responses to individual items on a sub-test of a battery the teacher can determine strengths and weaknesses of individuals and of classes or groups.

4. Counseling and guidance. Among the "tools" available to and used by the counselor, tests are often regarded as of central importance. Counselors frequently use measures of intelligence, achievement, aptitudes, interests, and personality to help pupils in counseling about careers, educational plans, and personal adjustment.

5. Marking. Teachers regularly use tests and examinations of their own devising as a basis for marking and grading, especially when measuring achievement in subject matter. However, tests of capacity such as the intelligence test are also useful in marking in that they provide a basis for judging whether or not a pupil is working up to capacity.

6. Curriculum evaluation. Both standardized and teacher-made tests are frequently used in attempts to evaluate various curricular offerings. Previous emphasis, for example, has been given to the setting up of objectives prior to instruction and the subsequent formulation of tests based on these objectives to indicate the extent to which these objectives have been met. Standardized tests, based on high content validity are also used.

7. Motivation. It is generally assumed that the prospect of taking a test motivates pupils to study. There is no doubt that most people make some preparation, if they can, when faced with the prospect of taking a final examination in a course. The use of tests for motivation is confined largely and quite naturally to achievement tests. There is little than an individual can or should do beforehand in trying to improve his score on tests of intelligence, aptitude, interests, or personality.

8. Identification and study of exceptional children. For those who are exceptional intellectually, tests have been found over many years to provide the best basis for screening and identification of both gifted and retarded. The procedure that seems most effective is to use group tests of mental ability along with nominations by teachers as the initial basis for screening. Those thus located are then tested with individual standardized tests usually administered by counselors or school psychologists.

9. Interpreting schools to the community. School
administrators are often asked to justify what schools
are doing and to present evidence that these objectives
are, in fact, being achieved. When citizens ask for
evidence on what their children are learning, the
results of testing programs are usually among the first
lines of evidence to be presented. Likewise, if the
question has to do with how well the schools are
achieving the objectives set up by and for them, test
scores provide evidence on this matter.

10. Improvement of school staff. The use of tests and
other measuring techniques can contribute substantially
to the professional development of teachers in several
ways: (a) putting on a measurement program can result in professional growth through the cooperative
planning, organizing, and conducting of such a project;
(b) the construction of tests and other methods for
local use can aid the teacher in identifying objectives
of instruction; (c) by giving the teacher insight into
the individual pupil's capacities, interests, achievements, personality problems, and needs.

11. Educational research. In school surveys, which are
often conducted for research purposes, tests are
useful tools for studying such problems as the
grade placement of pupils, achievement in basic
fundamentals, the relationship of the offerings of
the school to the needs of the community, and the
degree of success attained in realizing the educational
goals of the school or community. Tests may also serve
research purposes in the schools in conjunction with
comparative studies of different methods of teaching.

Cronbach (1963) makes specific suggestions for the uses
of tests and other measurements at both the elementary and high
school levels. At the elementary school level he discusses
their use in the areas of basic skills and concepts and social-
emotional development:

> Basic Skills and Concepts. In the elementary
> school, one aim is the development of the so-
> called fundamental skills of reading, quanti-
> tative thinking, and communication. Most of
> the teachers' evidence comes from observation
> of daily performance. Standardized tests are
> used occasionally for accurate measurement of
> these abilities. The better tests are designed

to measure understanding rather than mechanical performance. Questions about reading try to determine whether the pupils grasped the sense of the story ("Why did the Indians fight Daniel Boone?") rather than whether they simply followed the words ("What was Peter's sister called?"). Arithmetic skill is best tested with problems that require understanding of numerical relations rather than routine computations. Speed tests are used to appraise skills that should have reached a near-automatic level, but most authorities recommend that demand for speed be delayed until understanding is well developed.

Diagnostic evaluation is of great importance. Though special diagnostic tests are available, the teacher relies heavily on observations. He watches the pupil or asks him to solve the problems aloud. Thus he can note faulty processes that would not be clear in the written product. He discovers that one child seems mostly to need confidence, since he makes few errors when he plugs away step by step. Another is misled by the cue phrase "How much is left?" and tries to subtract when a percentage problem requires division. Still another is tripping himself by writing 4's that look like 7's. Similar analysis is made for reading, speech and writing.

Social-Emotional Development. The teacher can observe interests, attitudes, and social development. The choices pupils make when given free time, the ideas they contribute to a discussion, and the materials they display to others in the class are all indications of preferences and special interests. This means that the teacher who gives pupils the freedom to make choices will learn the most about them. Social learning and social difficulties are displayed continually. When the pupils are free to move around and interact, the teacher may observe helpfulness, leadership, supportive behavior, and conflict. Jimmy wants his own way. Carol is belligerent when tired. This is evidence on social growth and social needs, but such evidence is not at all standardized.

Emphasis should be placed on the integration of all information into a value judgment and a plan

for action. A low score in arithmetic might by
itself seem to say that immediate concentration
here is urgently required. Seeing this in relation to other facts, the teacher might conclude
that the pupil is at this time making rapid strides
toward gaining acceptance by the group and that play-
fulness during the arithmetic period is, for the
moment, a good sign. A very fine performance in
drawing might in one child be something to encourage; in another child, the result would
suggest a one-sided interest. Persistence we
normally regard as healthy, but when a usually
perfectionist student gives up on some half-
done project, this may be a good sign. He may
be seeing his efforts in better perspective.
(pp. 567-568)

Cronbach also suggests the following with respect to the
use of tests and other measurements at the high school level:

In high school, the responsibility for evaluation is divided among many teachers, and there is
some risk that no one will obtain a comprehensive view of the pupil. Individual teachers
judge progress in a particular subject, and the
more expert teachers will consider a wide range
of objectives in that evaluation. But evaluation of performance not peculiarly pertinent
to one particular subject (e.g., work habits)
is likely to be overlooked, and important questions about the relations among the pupil's
various achievements may not be asked.
The tests used for guidance, such as interest
tests, measures of adjustment, sociometric tests,
and tests of reading and study skills, also tell
about the effectiveness of instruction. Teachers
can observe important facts about adjustment and
intellectual functioning. When these data are
brought together where the teachers, counselors,
and administrators can and will use them, they
answer many questions and raise others. For example, it will be seen that many boys are developing
interests along scientific lines, but that none
is developing interest in writing or art. This
implies that the school program is failing to
reach and stimulate those boys who might develop
artistic or literary talents.

Guidance at its best is not restricted to a few hurried decisions. It is the process of appraising needs and readiness, and helping the pupil to understand what he is like and what he can do for himself. Seen in this way, guidance is inseparable from evaluation. An administrative structure that leaves guidance to a "guidance department" and expects evaluation to be done within each classroom misses the best possibilities of both.

Too often, test results are used only in the course for which the test was designed. They are not used by the pupil's other teachers during the same year or later. It is better if the science teacher learns what trouble the pupil has had in mathematics. The English teacher ought to find out which students are using language effectively in other subjects. Recording a grade in the office will not circulate this type of information. Ideally, each teacher will file a statement on each pupil, commenting on any significant characteristics noted.

Common practice falls far short of the ideal, both in breadth of evaluation and in use of results. If measurement is intended to obtain marks for administrative purposes, better evalution would not lead to many changes. We take the larger view that evaluition is an essential part of learning and of educational planning. It then follows that improved evaluation is the key to a more effective school. (p. 569)

REPORTING PUPIL PROGRESS

Once evaluations have been made by the classroom teacher, it is essential that he consider various factors in reporting the results to pupils, parents and other interested persons. Wrinkle (1956) has suggested the following factors which should be considered by teachers in marking and reporting:

1. The statement of any outcome or objective to be evaluated should be analyzed into its specific meanings so that its meaning is clearly stated.

2. The number of different forms should be kept at a minimum. If two or more short forms are to be used at the same time, they should be incorporated into a single form.

3. During a period of experimentation, unless there is plenty of money to spend on printing, forms should be produced by some inexpensive process such as mimeographing. An expensive printed form is less likely to be discarded even if it is known to be inadequate.

4. The basis for an evaluation of the student's achievement should be decided upon. Should the evaluation be in terms of established norms, the class average, or the ability of the student?

5. In the interpretation of a report the likelihood of misunderstanding by parents tends to increase in proportion to the number of details included in the report.

6. Students should have a real part in the development of new forms and practices.

7. The development by students of an understanding of and a favorable attitude toward new practices is a most effective approach to parent education.

8. The student's experiences, his successes, difficulties, abilities, and inabilities, should be the subject of frequent conversations between teacher and student. Students should be encouraged to take the initiative in asking for such conferences.

9. The summarization of reports on a student in a departmentalized program by a guidance counselor, a home-room teacher, a core teacher, or the principal involves too big a task and is not a workable plan.

10. Reporting on all students at one time during the school year is chiefly for the purpose of stimulating competitive comparisons; if such stimulation is not a purpose of the reporting, then reports should be made at different times to discourage such invidious comparisons.

11. The scale type evaluation form is unsatisfactory unless each scale item involves only a single outcome, the achievement of which can be expressed in degrees by clearly distinguishable descriptions.

12. The check form is simpler than the scale for use in

reporting evaluations and is more economical of
space on a printed form.

13. The development of highly detailed, elaborate cumulative record forms is uneconomical; if too detailed
and lengthy, they will not be used by most teachers.

14. To ensure an adequate understanding by parents of the
status of the student, a conference should be
arranged between the parents and the counselor or
teacher for the discussion of individual cases.

15. Although it has many real advantages, the conference
plan is not a practical solution to the reporting
problem, especially at the secondary-school level.

16. Check lists utilizing the best features of the
scale-type evaluation, the anecdotal record, and the
conference plan should be developed for the evaluation
of (a) general outcomes with which the total school
program is concerned and (b) more specific outcomes
relating to each of the various areas of the curriculum.

17. Parents should be sent a summary form of evaluation
focusing attention on desired outcomes of the school
program which have been analyzed in detail by the
check lists. The evaluation made should involve
cooperative activity on the part of students and
teachers.

18. Whatever forms for use in reporting are developed, a
separate report involving the use of a five-point
scale should be maintained for administrative record
purposes. Administrative records should not be confused by shifting from A B C D F to H S U to H M L
or other sets of symbols.

19. Check forms, unless they are carefully controlled,
tend to become increasingly detailed and, therefore,
increasingly impractical.

20. The best way to state objectives is in terms of desired behavior outcomes - what the learner should do.

21. Many teachers have difficulty in writing effective
comments. A deliberate program for the improvement
of the writing of informal comments is essential.

22. The most intelligible way to write supplementary comments in explaining evaluations is to tell what the student did.

Kingston and Wash (1966) have summarized the recommendations in the research literature on reporting to parents:

1. Assessments of attitudes, conduct, and citizenship should not be part of the evaluative marks in content areas.

2. Comments by teachers on specific weaknesses and strengths of students have been reported to enhance children's learning. Positive rather than negative comments are most beneficial.

3. Work samples which illustrate a child's skills, accompanied by an explanatory note from the teacher, can promote parents' understanding of marks and school objectives, particularly in the very early school years.

4. Report cards should give enough information to convey the child's status, but they should be functional enough to allow the teacher to mark the student objectively. The more entries appearing on a report card, and the greater the range of child behavior covered, the more likely it seems to be that the report card will meet the objectives and definitions of the marking system.

5. Dual reporting systems seem to have advantages in providing a more useful picture of the child's status and progress.

6. Informal letters and parents' conferences enhance the school-parent relationship.

7. No single system of marking seems to be adequate for reporting; a combination of reporting devices is desirable. (pp. 36-40)

An effective, but perhaps time consuming, method for reporting the results of evaluation to parents is through the parent conference. Johnson (1966) makes the following suggestions for the classroom teacher's preparing for parent conferences:

204

1. By collecting significant data about each child. Such
    data might include:
    a. Samples of the child's work on which the teacher
        has noted his evaluation. These might be a
        language story, arithmetic problems, a spelling
        list, etc.
    b. Textbooks and workbooks that the child is using.
    c. Booklets or special projects made by the student.
    d. Record of spelling words learned or new vocabu-
        lary acquired.
    e. Test results.
    f. Progress charts of various kinds.
    g. Summary reports.
    h. Tape recordings of class activities, etc.

2. By being organized. The teacher should have all
    materials organized and ready before the conference
    begins. By using a parent-teacher conference "prepa-
    ration" sheet, the teacher can record all significant
    information for discussion with the parents. The
    conference preparation sheet serves as a guide for
    conducting the conference.

3. By reviewing notes taken at previous conferences.
    After every conference, the teacher should jot down
    significant information, about the conference –
    parental reaction to suggestions, reaction to the
    school, acceptance of the child, willingness to
    cooperate, etc. Such notes are useful in preparing
    for each oral conference.

4. By staging an oral conference "rehearsal." There
    is no substitute for a couple of "dry runs" for both
    the experienced and inexperienced teacher. A tape
    recorder can be most helpful in pointing out the weak
    areas of the oral conference. Surprisingly, most
    teachers enjoy practicing on a colleague.

5. By checking the physical environment. An attractive
    classroom that reflects good teaching practices will
    help set the tone for a positive oral conference.
    Good housekeeping pays dividends, too.

6. By having a conference plan of "attack." Briefly
    stated, the following elements should be part of the
    teacher's "attack" plan.
    a. Establish rapport – greet the parents at the door,
        tour the room, "set the tone."

b. Have a positive beginning.
c. Don't do all the talking; encourage parents to talk.
d. Sincerely listen to what the parents say.
e. Develop the "we together" attitude of mutual cooperation.
f. Go easy on making lots of suggestions to the parents.
g. Draw the parents out and encourage suggestions from them.
h. Use the suggestions of parents as a springboard for action.
i. Be sure to summarize the points covered.
j. Make plans together for what is to happen in the future.
k. End on a positive note of continuing cooperation.
l. Make notes after the parents leave.
m. Follow through, follow through, follow through!!! (pp. 48-50)

The preceding discussion on reporting the results of evaluation should not lead the reader to imply that reporting these results to pupils are of secondary importance and that reporting to parents is of primary importance. The teacher should continuously strive to provide the pupil with continuous feedback with respect to his performance. These should be done as often as possible through report cards, periodic verbal feedback, and the rapid feedback of results on tests. It is only through such procedures that the classroom teacher can truly measure and evaluate pupil progress.

References

Adams, G. S., *Measurement and Evaluation in Education, Psychology and Guidance*, (New York: Holt, Rinehart, and Winston, 1964).

Ahmann, J. S. and Glock, M. D., *Evaluating Pupil Growth: Principles of Tests and Measurement*, (Boston: Allyn and Bacon, Inc., 1967).

Biehler, R. F., *Psychology Applied to Teaching*, (Boston: Houghton Mifflin Co., 1971).

_____, *Psychology Applied to Teaching*, (Dallas: Houghton Mifflin Co., 2nd Edition, 1974).

Blood, D. F. and Budd, W. C., *Educational Measurement and Evaluation*, (New York: Harper and Row Publishers, 1972).

Bloom, B. (ed.), *Taxonomy of Educational Objectives, Handbook I: Cognitive Domain*, (New York: Longmans, Green and Co., 1956).

Brown, F. G., *Principles of Educational and Psychological Testing*, (Hinsdale, Illinois: The Dryden Press, Inc., 1970).

Buros, O. K. (ed.), *The Seventh Mental Measurements Yearbook*, (Highland Park, New Jersey: Gryphon Press, 1972).

Chase, C. I., *Measurement for Educational Evaluation*, (Reading, Massachusetts: Addison - Wesley Publishing Co., 1974).

Cronbach, L. J., *Educational Psychology*, (New York: Harcourt, Brace, and World, Inc., 2nd Edition, 1963).

DeBlassie, R. R., "The Elementary School Cumulative Record: A Case Study in Miniature," *National Catholic Guidance Conference Journal*, 1971, 2, 143-146.

Diederich, P. B., *Shortcut Statistics for Teacher-Made Tests*, (Princeton, New Jersey: Educational Testing Service, 1964).

Dizney, H., *Classroom Evaluation for Teachers*, (Dubuque, Iowa: William C. Brown Co., 1971).

Douglas, L. M., The Secondary Teacher at Work, (Boston: D. C. Heath & Co., 1967).

Downie, N. M. and Heath, R. W., Basic Statistical Methods, (New York: Harper and Row Publishers, 3rd Edition, 1970)

Dressel, P. L., "Evaluation as Instruction," Proceedings of the 1953 Invitational Conference on Testing Problems, (Princeton, New Jersey: Educational Testing Service, 1954).

Ebel, R. L., "Improving the Competence of Teachers in Educational Measurement," The Clearing House, 1961, 36, 67-71.

_____, Measuring Educational Achievement, (Englewood Cliffs, New Jersey: Prentice-Hall, Inc., 1965).

Freeman, F. S., Theory and Practice of Psychological Testing, (New York: Holt, Rinehart, and Winston, 3rd Edition, 1962).

French, J. W. and Michael, W. B., Standards for Educational and Psychological Tests and Manuals, (Washington, D.C.: American Psychological Association, Inc., 1966).

Froehlich, C. and Hoyt, K., Guidance Testing, (Chicago: Science Research Associates, Inc., 1959).

Garrett, H. E., Statistics in Psychology and Education, (New York: David McKay Co., Inc., 6th Edition, 1966).

Gibson, R. L. and Higgins, R. E., Techniques of Guidance: An Approach to Pupil Analysis, (Chicago: Science Research Associates, 1966).

Green, J. A., Teacher-Made Tests, (New York: Harper and Row Publishers, 1963).

_____, Introduction to Measurement and Evaluation, (New York: Dodd, Mead, and Co., 1970).

Gronlund, N. E., Sociometry in the Classroom, (New York: Harper and Row, 1959).

_____, Measurement and Evaluation in Teaching, (New York: The Macmillan Co., 1971).

Harrington, W. E., A Study Guide for Measurement, (Dubuque, Iowa: William C. Brown, Publishers, 1969).

Hedges, W. D., Evaluation in the Elementary School, (New York: Holt, Rinehart, and Winston, Inc., 1969).

Horvocks, J. E. and Schoonover, T. I., Measurement for Teachers, (Columbus: Charles E. Merrill Publishing Co., 1968).

Johnson, W. R., "Parent-Teacher Conferences," The National Elementary Principal, 1966, 45, 48-50.

Kibler, R., Barker, L., and Miles, D. T., Behavioral Objectives and Instruction, (Boston: Allyn and Bacon, Inc., 1970).

Kingston, A. J. and Wash, Jr., J. A., "Research on Reporting Systems," The National Elementary Principal, 1966, 45, 36-40.

Krathwohl, D. R., Bloom, B. S., and Masia, B. B., Taxonomy of Educational Objectives, The Classification of Educational Goals, Handbook II: Affective Domain, (New York: David McKay, 1964).

Kuder, G. F. and Richardson, M. W., "The Theory of the Estimation of Test Reliability," Psychometrika, 1937, 2, 151-260.

Lien, A. J., Measurement and Evaluation of Learning, (Dubuque, Iowa: William C. Brown Co., 1971).

Lindeman, R. H., Educational Measurement, (Glenview, Illinois: Scott, Foresman and Co., 1967).

Marshall, J. C. and Hales, L. W., Classroom Test Construction, (Reading, Massachusetts: Addison-Wesley Publishing Co., 1971).

_____, Essentials of Testing, (Reading, Massachusetts: Addison-Wesley Publishing Co., 1972).

Michaelis, J. U., Social Studies for Children in a Democracy, (Englewood Cliffs, New Jersey: Prentice-Hall, Inc., 1963).

_____, and Karnes, M. R., Measuring Educational Achievement, (New York: McGraw-Hill Book Co., 1950).

Plowman, P. D., Behavioral Objectives, (Chicago: Science Research Associates, 1971).

Remmers, H. H., Gage, N. L., and Rummel, J. F., A Practical Introduction to Measurement and Evaluation, (New York: Harper & Brothers Publishers, 1960).

Shertzer, B. and Stone, S. C., Fundamentals of Guidance, Boston: Houghton Mifflin Co., 1966).

_____, Fundamentals of Guidance, (Boston: Houghton Mifflin Co., 2nd Edition, 1971).

Smith, F. M. and Adams, S., Educational Measurement for the Classroom Teacher, (New York: Harper and Row Publishers, 1966).

Stanley, J. C., Measurement in Today's Schools, (Englewood Cliffs, New Jersey: Prentice-Hall, Inc., 1964).

Storey, A. G., The Measurement of Classroom Learning, (Chicago: Science Research Associates, 1970).

Thorndike, R. L. and Hagen, E., Measurement and Evaluation in Psychology and Education, (New York: John Wiley and Sons, Inc., 1969).

Tiedeman, H. R., Fundamentals of Psychological and Educational Measurement, (Springfield, Illinois: Charles C. Thomas Publishers, 1972).

Tinkelman, S. N., "Planning the Objective Test," in R. L. Thorndike, editor, Educational Measurement, (Washington, D. C.: American Council on Education, 2nd Edition, 1971).

Traxler, A. E., The Nature and Use of Anecdotal Records, (New York: Harper and Brothers, 1949).

_____, "Fundamentals of Testing," Test Service Notebook, No. 27, (New York: Harcourt, Brace, and World, Inc., 1962).

Wrinkle, W. L., Improving Marking and Reporting Practices in Elementary and Secondary Schools, (New York: Rinehart, 1956).